FATHER NATURE

AMERICAN LAND & LIFE SERIES

Edited by Wayne Franklin

FATHER NATURE

Fathers as Guides to the Natural World

EDITED BY PAUL S. PIPER *&* STAN TAG

UNIVERSITY OF IOWA PRESS : IOWA CITY

University of Iowa Press, Iowa City 52242

Copyright © 2003 by the University of Iowa Press

Printed in the United States of America

Design by Richard Hendel

http://www.uiowa.edu/uiowapress

The publication of this book was generously supported by the University of Iowa Foundation.

Printed on acid-free paper

Library of Congress Cataloging-in-Publication Data
Father nature: fathers as guides to the natural world / edited
by Paul S. Piper and Stan Tag.
p.   cm.—(American land and life series)
ISBN 0-87745-846-4 (cloth), ISBN 0-87745-837-5 (pbk.)
1. Fathers.   2. Father and child.   3. Outdoor recreation.
4. Nature study.   I. Tag, Stan, 1962–   .   II. Series.
HQ756.F38244 2003
306.874′2—dc21   2002075075

03   04   05   06   07   C   5   4   3   2   1
03   04   05   06   07   P   5   4   3   2   1

To our fathers,

Charles and Roger,

and to our children,

Jordan, Arwen, and

Ruth

CONTENTS

FOREWORD
Wayne Franklin

In ways that modernists and postmodernists alike rarely acknowledge, our culture is the profound heir of the Romantic reaction against older modes of thought and feeling. Take the case of what we call "nature." That concept certainly predates the Romantics. The word itself, after all, is of Latin origin, with roots in ancient notions of generation and nativity. Nature for the Romans was both the innermost signature of a thing or being and, more abstractly, the source of life, the principle of the universe as an organic entity. While our own attitudes toward nature surely incorporate many such classical assumptions, in various ways our concepts are surprisingly recent. We tend to think of nature, for instance, as in some sense the outer sign of the soul's alienation from the confinements and corruptions of society, an idea only vaguely present in pre-Romantic views. In its eagerness to find some ground for the self separate from the social world, Romanticism took nature as a proper site of the individual's spiritual quest.

Few motifs are more common in Romantic literature than the one that situates an injured self in a natural domain where the sounds of human activity fade and more beneficent influences begin to restore health and sanity.

This mythology of nature as the proper home of the human self has had extraordinary consequences over the past two centuries. The designation of park land and preserves owes much to the dawning of environmental and ecological thought. Surely part of our gradually developing motive has been to set aside places where nature, relatively unaffected by our own activity, could find its own health. But at the outset the park movement more clearly drew on, and in turn reinforced, the notion that the human soul needs sparsely settled spaces in which to roam. Henry David Thoreau himself, in first articulating his vision of what he called "our natural preserves," spoke of their highest use as "our own true re-creation."

When we think of nature in these terms we tend to overlook those purposes that nature—in our complete absence—serves, and will continue to serve, unto itself. We also tend to miss how socially constructed our experience of the natural world today is. The very designation of Thoreau's "preserves" across the latter part of the nineteenth century was the result of tough political fights that among other things gave natural areas some standing within the prevailing codes of human law. Setting aside such areas made them perforce part of our maps in ways that truly wild nature never is. They were claimed and bounded and occupied in Yellowstone and Yosemite as much as they were "preserved." And around such parcels of nature as these there sprang up an elaborate economy that included several substantial cultural industries. Paintings by the likes of Albert Bierstadt inspired awe of nature but they also helped to shape tourist itineraries. They packaged nature as the place one went in order to find oneself. The railroads and hotels were happy to serve this spiritual longing by selling their material services.

But there are more subtle ways in which nature is profoundly our own artifact. Romanticism would have us believe that the urge to throw ourselves into nature is instinctual and ancient. To the contrary, we would do well to recall how much of our attitude toward nature and our place in it is learned. The propaganda of the railroads (and later, of the auto manufacturers) played on the Romantic desire to leave "the world" behind and enter a realm of primal beauty and energy. In the process, the propaganda promised renewal. While such popular documents and images as tourist brochures and advertisements and prints and photos almost always suggested that the renewal came by breaking with society, the activity promoted was itself part of a massive social movement. And it was as much a part of the economy as the things that tied individuals to "the world" in the first place. In driving the Going-to-the-Sun Highway in Glacier National Park following its completion in 1933, the auto tourist was much more likely to be a compliant consumer than a venturesome rebel.

If nature is an obvious human product in such landscapes, in other ways its construction is more nuanced. We are propagandized by entities wishing to separate us from our socially validated money as they pretend to separate us from society. But in fact, as the present volume reveals, we also learn about our ties to nature by means less directly connected to the marketplace. *Father Nature* gathers a collection of surprising reflections on how modern American fathers have instructed their children to take their proper place in nature. Much of the book shows the means by which outdoor activities that Henry David Thoreau himself recognized as useful entrees to the natural world are replicated across the generations. Hunting, fishing, and trapping are chief among them. The book thus documents a kind of nature education that has been going on for a very long time. These are, in origin and often in their modern details, deeply traditional crafts. Thoreau in *A Week on the Concord and Merrimack* represents fishermen as among the ancient fixtures of nature itself, practicing their craft not as a "sport, nor solely a means of subsistence, but a sort of solemn sacrament and withdrawal from the world." In almost every instance in *Father Nature*, such traditional activities are also colored by these same Romantic assumptions. The point of the education is at times quite practical, but usually the issue is not subsistence. It is spiritual health, a sense of belonging to some community above and beyond the ordinary ones where (as the memoirs printed here also often show us) the teachers and their pupils dwell. That so many of these now adult children have such warm memories of their tutelage suggests a good deal about the role fathers play in passing on knowledge and values to their daughters and sons. That is in itself an important aspect of the volume. But nature is the lesson as well as the classroom here. "Thus, by one bait or another," as Thoreau says of the fishermen he encounters, "Nature allures inhabitants into all her recesses."

This book itself, even as it documents a myriad of family relationships and acquires real interest by doing so, is also a kind of bait. Reading it, one wants to take one more stroll in the woods with the perpetually young child of a parent's idealistic imagination. Here is nature as we may long to know it, nature as we may wish to introduce it to those who will walk and hunt and reverence it and themselves, we may hope, long after we are gone.

ACKNOWLEDGMENTS

Paul: To my mother, Winnifred Piper, who graciously pushed my father and me out the door toward northward lakes and rivers; to my father, Charles, who gave me an intense love and reverence for the natural world with its many faces; to Joan, my wife, for her love and encouragement in ways too numerous to count; to Frank Stewart for his ongoing discussions, faith, and advice; to Kate Trueblood for endless energy, endless ideas, and endless encouragement; and to Rick Newby, dear friend, and Deb Clow, my favorite editor, for logistics and Montana vibes.

Stan: My father, Roger, once wrote part of a novel, and in that I found inspiration to begin a lifetime of writing. Generously, he allowed me to quote extensively from his letters, and he has been deeply supportive of my writing and my life. I also want to thank my mother, Judy, for her love and encouragement, and mostly for taking my sister, brother, and me outside: to the beaches, the desert, the mountains, and to the redwoods, Yellowstone, Big Bear, Crater Lake, and many other marvelous places. My mother's love for gardens and sand and rivers and sunshine lives in me. I am especially thankful that she put me in Boy Scouts, where I escaped the city, learned to hike and camp and roam the Sierras, and where I found men who became second fathers to me. In their own quirky and genuine ways, these men taught me how to endure, how to enjoy the chill of morning in the high mountains and icy plunges into tarns, how to become a leader, and how to accept my small place on this planet. I hope some of them will read this book and know how much it means to boys and girls to be led outward from the often maddening confines of their own young lives into the world itself: mysterious, marvelous, wild. Thanks also to Sylvia for reading "Hellgrammite Dance" so carefully. Her insights led to many improvements. It has been a joy learning to be a father to Arwen and Ruth with Sylvia as spouse, partner, and the best mother two girls could ever have.

We would also like to thank all the writers who contributed their essays to this book, Wayne Franklin for his helpful suggestions and support, and the Bureau for Faculty Research at Western Washington University for their generous grants.

Our fathers took us outside. They were our guides to worlds of sun and wind, water and ice, plant and rock. They taught us to skip smooth stones over the surface of lakes, and to find trout by reading the riffles and pools of rivers. But more than that, they taught us how to slow down and pay attention to the marvels of nature. They taught us silence. This is where the seeds for this book began to take root. Exploring the natural world with our fathers evoked in us deep questions about existence, origins, beauty, and change. And it forged deep relationships as well. These questions and relationships are at the heart of *Father Nature*.

During our initial conversations about editing a book of personal essays on fathers and nature, we wondered what roles other fathers had played in fostering connections and intimacy between their children and the natural world. How prevalent was it? How diverse? While fathers have been justly criticized for their absence from families, and for their abuse of partners and children, this is not all fathers, nor all that fathers are. For this book we sought stories of fathers as guides into the natural world, both in action and perception. Fathers who revealed what was real and sacred to them. Fathers who shared the way a river slipped whispering around a bend, the way a serrated ridge defined sky, or the way an isolated stretch of shoreline created an ache in their soul. Fathers who studied birds, and who let children eat dirt. These were the kinds of stories we began to gather. The essays that came to us, however, were not simplistic, and often exposed complexities and paradox, for fathering well is often difficult and challenging in ways that may never be mastered or understood.

What ultimately ties these essays together is a fierce love between fathers and their children, and the need to express this love in the experience of nature. These essays explore the essence of being a father, of having a father, and of losing a father. They explore the landscapes of love, death, belonging, wonder, contact, recovery, identity, hope, coming-of-age, and succession, as well as lessons taught by animals, trees, mountains, rivers, and ice.

The eighteen essays in *Father Nature* are arranged into three sections followed by a coda. The first section, "Fathers," contains essays by daughters and sons about their fathers and the ways these fathers shaped their children's lives and perceptions of nature. There are fathers who fish, hunt, and trap—certainly the kinds of fathers and experiences one would expect in such a collection—but also fathers who are university professors and yard landscapers; fathers who are absent, cruel, or silent; fathers who love only the harshest landscapes; and fathers who take their children into tide-pools and redwood groves.

The second section, "Fathers and Fathering," is transitional, linking the reflections on fathers to the experience of fathering. What does it mean, these essays ask, to be both son and father at the same time? How do our experiences with our fathers shape the fathers we become, how we treat our children, and what we teach them (or they teach us) about nature? What are the ritualistic, cultural, and biological transformations we make from being sons to becoming fathers? How do our experiences with our children reshape how we understand and relate to our own fathers? What lessons does nature offer us in considering such successions?

The third section, "Fathering," explores more fully the challenges, dilemmas, and rewards of fathering itself. These essays are arranged chronologically by the age of the children, youngest to oldest, and reflect developmental stages from infancy to young adulthood. What does it mean to be a father who loves the natural world and who wants his children to share his sense of wonder and curiosity? What happens when children show little interest in such things, and even declare that nature is boring? What does it mean to see the world through the eyes of a child? What do fathers learn from their children's discoveries, revelations, and life in nature?

The coda brings this book full circle: a daughter considering the significance of the life and death of her father, and her father's love of nature, on her own life. How do any of us live with the loss of our fathers, their absence, and the ways they continue to nurture our lives? Life, death, and rebirth circulate through this book, as they circulate through our lives as parents, as children, as humans, and as creatures of nature who inhabit this mysterious, fascinating, and sometimes terrifying planet whirling through space.

It is with great hope for the future that we have gathered these essays together. May they inspire and guide. If we, as editors, have learned anything in the course of putting this book together, it is that a relationship with nature is not just a relationship with a forest or river or animal; it is a relationship with the core of our being. We are all children of nature in its marvelous complexity and contradiction. It is simply up to us to realize it and, as parents, to open the door for our own children and let them wander outside.

FATHERS

Her Father's Daughter

How do you thank the person who gave you a vantage from which to see the world?

The water in my cup of sea-vegetable tonic is the color of the Pacific Ocean in June, gone green beneath low southern California beach clouds. In its pretty murk I see the bay at the bottom of the cliff we hiked down a hundred Sunday mornings in the late 1950s, all for the love of fishing and tide-pools.

The cliff path ended at Bluff Cove, an off-center half-moon of cold green water. Its right curve rose onto a pocked granite plateau that became a rocky peninsula aimed straight out into the sea. When the tide was out, the plateau was transformed into a landscape of child-sized seawater lakes. That was when our father would light a cigarette and station himself on the end of the gun barrel of the westernmost rock that held that particular piece of Pacific ransom. He wanted its rockfish—its coppers and cow cod—and he would stand out there all day like the sight on a rifle, firing his baited bullet into the boiling target while the surf shot back at him, encircling his form again and again with frothy shrapnel, then salty haloes, as if he were an angel for having daughters, not sons, and not regretting it.

It was our good luck that he didn't differentiate and just went ahead and taught us to do the things he'd learned to love as a boy in New Zealand—fishing, hiking, camping, and exploring the coastal biologies of the Pacific. While our father fished, my sister and I played in the tide-pools, a sport we never tired of. Our father had taught us the secret: Move too fast and you miss it all; sit still and the thing comes to life. It was riveting work, peering like God into whole watery worlds, on the lookout for tiny, heavily camouflaged sculpin; hermit crabs masquerading as dwarf olive snails; even baby octopuses. We made gleeful games of poking pastel-tentacled sea anemones, retrieving our fingers the moment we felt their terrifying sucking. We watched in amazement as purple sea urchins waved their spines in slow motion as they inched along the rock, and we feigned extreme mortification when our father suggested we actually eat their squishy, persimmon-colored roe, his favorite seaside snack.

Then there was always the business of shell collecting, still prosperous in the southern California of the late '50s: rough-ribbed nerites with their dear little baby teeth, keyhole limpets for future necklaces, abalone shells in their opaline beauty, apricot California cones, dunce-cap turrets, spotted cowries, and our family favorite, the handsome Maxwell murexes. In those years there was no doubt that our father had delivered us into a natural state of grace, and we loved him for it.

If you dig around in the familial soil of almost anyone who feels close to the natural world, you're likely to find good rootstock, a parent or grandparent, an uncle, maybe family friends, who made it their responsibility to introduce the children in their lives to life out-of-doors. The indelible power of these natural mentors deserves serious consideration. It's safe to say, for my part, anyway, that I most certainly wouldn't be writing this had it not been for the early influence of my father; wouldn't, perhaps, ever have done anything with a conservationist's passion had he not personally initiated me into the great masterworks of nature.

How would I see the world today had I never witnessed dozens of navy blue snakes dash over riverbed rocks in the California redwoods? Would I live now on a rural island in the Pacific Northwest if we hadn't camped along the Inside Passage's Ice Age archipelago when I was ten? Would a Japanese fish print, of my prize twenty-nine-pound salmon, hang above my bed had my father not baited countless oceangoing hooks for me before I ever left grammar school? Would I love nature the way I do? Would I need it like a vitamin? Believe wholly that I belong to it and insist on protecting it always?

There are no guarantees that children will pick up the scent and follow the trail, but if we want half a chance at turning out environmentally responsible people, for God's sake, get them out of the house.

Timothy Egan, *New York Times* northwestern correspondent and author of the elegant eco-manifesto *The Good Rain*, credits his grandfather with being "the guy who taught me how to land brook trout with a hand-tied fly."

Novelist and nature essayist Brenda Peterson pins her love of water, woods, and moose meat on her father, who worked for the Forest Service.

Guido R. Rahr III, a graduate student at Yale's School of Forestry and Environmental Studies, claims that his conservationist zeal began with his outdoorsman father, whose own father, a friend of Aldo Leopold, took him hiking everywhere. "We hiked the Oregon Deschutes, the Columbia River Gorge; we hiked up the Teton River in Montana and in the north woods of Wisconsin. Dad never said, 'You will love nature.' He just took us along. And it worked."

For my sister and me it was The Camping Trip. I was almost nine, she was seven, and somehow our father managed to get a whole month off from work and take us camping, from Santa Barbara to Vancouver Island. We traveled in Betsy, our father's tank of a Cadillac, which gracefully suffered the indignities of being both wedding-mint green and afflicted with chronic fuel-pump flatulence.

We caught smelt in Morro Bay, slept in the misted magnificence of the northern California coast, and watched the rain take Oregon. Driving slowly, stopping often as we went, that trip taught us what native people have always known: The land folds into itself as it goes and there are no lines, just the great green reach of nature.

How do you thank the person who set your compass straight so early? That's what I asked myself standing by my father's hospital bed in San Pedro, California, last May. He was dying—of failed lungs, now a failing heart, the last stage of emphysema. I knew his mind was on spiritual things. Every once in a while, like a feverish chant, he'd repeat to himself, "Jesus died to take away our sins." I wanted to discuss some bigger ideas.

Finally, after a day and a half of family visits, I found myself alone with my father. "You know, there's nothing to be afraid of," I began, feeling foolish. He patted my arm. The warmth of his hand startled me.

"I brought a book," I said. "There's a part I wanted to read to you." He nodded and struggled with a pillow. I began: "Psychiatrist Ann Linthorst says: 'We are not, in reality, hunks of life. Life . . . is one, nondimensional, spiritual substance to which we may awaken in consciousness. . . . We are not really persons, we are awarenesses.'"

"That's it!" my father cried out suddenly, pointing his right index finger heavenward. His eyes were wide open now. "That's it. I didn't know you knew."

And I certainly didn't know he did. He died in peace the following night. I was supposed to leave on an Alaska fishing trip the next morning, but I was too disoriented to pack, much less go. I spent the next two days in a fog. Then on Friday, May 29, I woke up early and strangely clearheaded. There was one seat left on one Alaska Airlines flight, which left in two hours.

It was a classic Northwest spring day, polished and blue, plum and apple trees in bloom on both sides of the road. At exactly 12:30 P.M., on the crest of my favorite hill, I looked up and there, as wide as the sky, was my father's face. It was translucent but utterly vivid, and smiling. And while I could see it up there, I could also feel it all around me. My first thought was, "Oh, God, this is like that Woody Allen movie!"

But it wasn't. It was some kind of honest vision, a heavenly hologram of the face I knew and loved, wearing an expression I'd never seen before in my life, on anyone. It was absent of all pain, all concern—radiant, beatific, ecstatic, indescribable. It was, it has to have been, divine.

Late that afternoon my sister called me in Juneau from our childhood beach town, where she still lives. She was breathless. "This is the most incredible day of my life!" she cried. "I saw Daddy in a vision!"

"Wait!" I interrupted. "Did you see his face in the sky, as big as the sky?"

"Yes!" she yelled. "He was beaming! He looked like the Buddha!"

At 3:30 P.M., while driving by herself, she had looked up and witnessed exactly what I had seen three hours earlier.

"What I saw was palpable. Like I could touch him. Then it suddenly shot into me, like in *Star Wars* when the camera zooms you in and suddenly you're *there*."

She had to turn a corner, so she waved and said, "Bye, Daddy! Bye!" but there he was again in the sky in the other direction, beaming.

That August, when we sailed across the South Bay toward our old tide-pooling grounds, my sister and I knew that the ashes in the metal box were the remains of our father's body, but not of him. Still, it was an eerie business. When the boat was as close to Bluff Cove as the currents would allow, we each took a breath, then took a handful of the lacy white ancestral grit.

"It looks like seashells!" my sister breathed. Indeed it did. It was bone chips, really; that's what cremation ashes are, mineral remnants of nature's structural engineering, the girding that lets a body stand . . . and cast a fishing line.

Our father's bones arced down the rolling green belly of the ocean like an underwater snowstorm. Soon they would be octopus beak, sardine spine, elegant Maxwell murexes, sea vegetables collected for health-food-store chlorophyll tonics designed to refresh the blood with ocean nutrition. In a few years our father's bones might nourish our own the way salmon carcasses leave behind sea minerals for their offspring in their spawning streams, one of nature's truest circles.

There's something to this cellular legacy, something that continues to circulate right on down the family line. Our father's father had been a marine biologist on the bonny banks of New Zealand, a shark specialist. And back at the hospital, when I asked our father the meaning of the word *Reviresco* on the Maxwell family crest, he smiled and said, "Forever green."

Traplines

My father remains a trapper. Even now, when he's long retired from his traplines, he sees animal tracks with a trapper's eyes, watches the willows along the Salmon River behind his house for the fresh toothmarks of beaver, and checks the price of fur if a fur-buying house sends one of their infrequent bulletins. The price of fur has been poor for decades now, so my father has less incentive to dream of his trapping days, when he was able to take Septembers, Octobers, and Novembers off from salaried jobs and walk the streambanks and logging roads of Sawtooth Valley and still make enough money to support a family.

He also isn't bothered by the innocent young men who once sought him out as a mentor. They would ask him to teach them to trap and he would tell them where and how to make sets for beaver, muskrat, bobcat, and coyote. He would skin and stretch what they caught and split the profits with them. Such partnerships usually lasted only a season or two, until the young men realized that the life they wanted to live was best lived in a different century, and the reason my father had been able to make life as a trapper practical was that he had other irons in the fire, sometimes literally: he was also a welder, blacksmith, and mechanic.

But he remains a trapper. He traps mice on his back porch, and the moles that puncture his lawn in the summer. He picks out spots where a trap could be concealed beneath the small paths made by mink along the river, and he spots the coyotes as they walk the hills around his house. At some level of memory, he wants to trap those coyotes, kill them, take them home and skin them and stretch their hides to dry over frames until the fur buyer comes through.

You might think that such desire would alienate him from the complex and not-human world that begins beyond our family's fencelines in Sawtooth Valley, but it hasn't. Near the end of his active trapping career, he spread a few traps along the trail on the other side of the river one fall and then watched as a storm covered them with two feet of snow. He left the traps there over the winter. It wasn't until the next July, when he was out wandering his pastures, that he had the thought that he ought to check them. He crossed the river and gathered up traps, all snow-sprung except one, which held a young coyote, fresh caught. Because it was summer and the coyote was small and its fur was worthless to the buyers, he put a pine branch across the coyote's neck, pinned it to the ground, released its leg from the trap, and stepped back to watch it run off.

I asked him what the coyote had looked like. "Happy," he said. But there was more to it than happy. He had been allowed into a world that the coyotes usually keep for themselves. That was the last time my father put out traps for any animal that didn't irritate him.

I don't trap. I grew up with trapping and hunting smells rising up from the cellar of our house: the sharp odors of stripped flesh and clotted blood, of gutted ducks and pheasants, of beaver scent glands and the rancid piles of fat scraped from hides. As a small child, when I had accompanied my father on his traplines, we had often come upon mink and marten and otter alive in his traps. I wanted to take them home as pets. They would hiss and scream and tear at the earth at the end of their chains. Then my father would kill them. I would make a fuss, and then I'd end up sitting in the pickup while he checked more traps.

I knew they were vicious little animals who had shown their prey no more compassion than my father showed them, but at age six it was tough to balance that knowledge against the Disney movies I had seen on a cousin's TV in Boise. Recently, when I read in a student paper the words "This story reminds me again that character is always shaped by cruel forces," I paused in my correcting for a moment and thought for the first time in months about that trapline.

My father tried to teach me to skin animals, but I was awkward with the knife. I sliced through the delicate hides or tore the fur on the wooden stretchers, eliminating not just traplines but medical school from my future. He had earlier tried to teach me to hunt, with more success. I had done well at that, killing probably sixteen deer by the time I was sixteen, at which point I said enough and quit hunting until I was thirty-nine.

At that advanced age, I consciously accepted my family's ethic that you ought to kill the meat you eat, and began killing animals again. But there had been twenty-odd years in which I hadn't been very conscious of my father's trapping or hunting, even though I had eaten a lot of venison chops and elk steak in that time and even though I had begun wearing—and still wear—a fur hat that my father had given me. It had been made from a beaver he had trapped. Once when a picture of that hat on my head showed up on the front page of a newspaper—I had been standing in an unemployment line—a woman wrote me a bitter letter about the cruelty of wearing fur. I thought about the complicated reply I would have to give her, one that would have to detail my family finances along with my family's values, and let her letter go unanswered.

But I did begin killing again. And the act of sighting a deer's ear through a rifle scope, putting the crosshairs on it, and pulling the trigger marked me as someone who had awakened, not just to a paradoxical combination of ethical itch and blood lust, but to the world I stood on. But it was not an awakening caused by the roar of my rifle or the sudden high pirouette of a head-shot buck. It was caused by something else altogether.

Just before my thirty-ninth birthday I had taken one of the small sheds on the ranch and put it on a trailer and wheeled it out near the river. I put it on a foundation of stilts, insulated it with four inches of Styrofoam in the floors and ceiling, and equipped it with a barrel stove that my father had welded up for me. When I was done I had created a heavy-duty, industrial-model sauna.

While I was cleaning that shed out before moving it, I pried a piece of Sheetrock from one of the inside walls and discovered, hanging on nails, a cache of beaver scent glands left over from my father's trapping days. He had sold ones like them to perfume companies for tens of dollars a pound in the early sixties. Of course, it took many beaver to make a pound of scent glands, but over most of his seasons he caught ninety or a hundred of them; so scent glands had amounted to an appreciable portion of his trapping income over the years.

These, however, had been walled up and forgotten. Altogether they made less than a pound. They were completely mummified, and the fragrant oil they had contained had sunk deep into the wood behind them. I took them off their nails and threw them in the burning pile, and a week later they were smoke.

I had paneled the inside of the sauna with cedar and built benches against the wall on either side of the stove. My girlfriend at the time was a psychotherapist, into archetypes and aromatherapy, and she brought two bunches of eucalyptus leaves that she hung from the ceiling above the stove. It was a cold day in November when we fired up the sauna for the first time. When the barrel stove was red-hot, I poured water from a bucket onto the bare metal. Great clouds of steam and eucalyptus oil began to bathe our bodies. Our sinuses snapped open. Within a few minutes, the candle in a wall mount had slumped over from the heat, and a thermometer near the roof read 160° F. A few minutes after that we dove out the door and into the Salmon River, where we stayed until heatstroke and eucalyptus overdose were no longer possibilities.

When we went back into the sauna to warm up again, we discovered a new smell. The heat had penetrated four inches of Styrofoam and volatilized the violent pheromones of the mummified rodent glands. A thick miasma of Eau de Beaver, sharpened by the odors of wet fresh cedar, eucalyptus, and sweat, all of it too hot to breathe without cooling it through the nose, was what passed for atmosphere in that sauna.

It was not unpleasant. It was the smell of home, of place, of where my heart was. It was not long after that I killed that first-in-a-long-time deer. Then my relationship with the therapist—who had smelled in the sauna creatures who lurked beyond her own psychic and olfactory fencelines—ended.

Out of these developments came others. I have married a woman who grew up on a cattle ranch, who has breathed air that carried the heavy scents of branded and castrated and butchered cows. I suspect we were brought together by our nasal receptors.

And I have reversed the process whereby I eat the wild meat that my father has hunted. Some years, I hunt and he eats. In moments of high optimism, I think that all these events are evidence that I'm growing up, which in my family—and everyone else's—means accepting and even embracing the cruel and absolute forces that have shaped all our characters. In moments of high pessimism I recognize the same thing.

Late this November I walked across the river from my sauna and climbed up the hillside until I sighted the small herd of elk that grazes there in the cold early mornings. I picked a cow elk out of the herd, found her rib cage in my cross hairs, and shot her. She fell to her knees, then struggled back to her feet and moved off into the trees. I tracked the blood trail for fifty yards and then spotted her standing in a small clearing. She fell to her knees again, then to her side, and then, as I approached, looked back over her shoulder at me, and died.

I spent the next hour gutting her. A cow elk is a big animal and I had forgotten a hoist. By the time I had gotten the intestines and heart and bullet-shattered lungs and windpipe out, I was covered with blood from my fingernails to my armpits. A dense mist rose from the carcass into the cold morning air.

The body cavity held an inch-deep lake of clotting blood that had to be cleaned out before it spoiled the meat. I pulled the hind legs over a log, and scooped blood out in double handfuls until the ground around me was soaked red. I propped the rib cage open with a pine branch so the carcass would cool out properly, picked up my rifle, and began walking home. Once there, I would put a pack saddle on the horse, and gather up knives, a saw, and game bags.

As I reached the brow of the hill that rises from the Salmon River, I was able to look down at my family's forty acres. The river marks its west side, the highway its east side. The fencelines north and south are marked by crossbuck fences, and from a distance look like markings on an old map. There, in that valley, at that moment, the place itself looked like it had been drawn onto a photograph, like its existence was only an inked-in one, and yet that ink—those structures, those marks, those lines—were what made it habitable, what made it human, what made it home.

I stood in and saw from the great wild for a moment, but then that vision faded and I saw only the solid single horse in the pasture, the houses and outbuildings and the sauna, the Xs of the crossbucks, the smoke from the chimneys, and the pickups of other hunters moving slowly on the highway. These are not things wild animals attend to, but they are the things that make up our world. That world holds us fast, and I'm not always sure it is worth the brutal surgeries one has to perform to escape it even for a moment.

So I walked down the hill to the river, watching the pasture get closer. Then a thought: This is where I will always live. And then its dark corollary: This is where I will die. And then one small and wild hope: someday the coyotes might let me out of this trap.

Around the Next Bend

A flood of memories, like the tide coming in blurring the current of the Samish River, clouding clear water and pushing schools of king salmon upstream to spawn. I watch my father's head drop, his arm slide off the arm of the couch, a book slip from his lap. This visit he is frailer. His face like an owl relief carved in worn rock. I wonder at this man who once held me aloft, in sky and sun, to look down on him. I feel sorrow, and my thoughts drift downstream.

Portaging the Basswood River in Quetico Park many years ago, a seventeen-foot aluminum canoe on his shoulders, a heavy canvas haversack on his back, another (mine) on his chest; no hands to swat away the squadrons of no-see-ums, blackflies, deerflies, and mosquitoes that hovered in the dead air under the canoe. I remember his labored breathing as I walked behind him carrying paddles and fishing rods. Ten years old, feeling like I was doing my part. He was the guide and I the child.

Yesterday I suggested we go out and wade a river, and he groaned under his breath. Sciatica made it difficult for him to walk, much less wade, and his balance has been failing for years. Scrambling into waders, rigging up a rod, fighting current and insects, and battling blackberries were no longer the transcendent joys they had once been. Yet he went, found a place to sit and cast some, and ate berries while I walked a mile of stream or so. And when I'd called him last week and told him about the king salmon I'd landed, he was as excited as I was. And I knew then that I kept fishing as much for him as for myself.

I have yet to learn all he taught me.

Patience. He could fish a small pool on Montana's Swan River for a half hour, changing lures, placing casts just inside the back eddy behind a deadfall spruce. I'd pass him and be fishing four holes ahead when I'd hear a whoop, and stumbling back in waders see him sliding his trophy onto the cobble. A wild rainbow or brookie, dazzling colors under the immense Montana sky.

Experimentation. He was a maverick. His clothes were usually secondhand. He favored bow ties and scorned fashion. The same was true of fishing. If the locals recommended Daredevils, he'd use spinners; if flies, he'd use spoons. He'd vary retrieves, locations, and if he didn't catch as many fish, well, so what? He did it his way.

Observation. He'd notice mice tunnels underfoot; warblers flitting in the willows; a beaver sliding under a cutbank; the way a leaf twisted to reveal a scarlet underbelly. He had a way with silence, and could listen well, which is still my measure of a good person. We would sit sometimes without fishing, without talking, and if I were still enough, the world would seem to suddenly emerge. Bird song, gusts of warm wind, the scent of cottonwood buds, of dogwood, the purr of water suddenly there.

Curiosity. We'd wander far beyond our plan, often struggling back downstream after dark. Many days we forgot lunch, and one day in particular on the Big Hole, we ate lunch around four in the afternoon sitting on a beaver dam. The peanut butter and jelly sandwiches had fused into balls of soggy sticky bread. Dinner would be a ten o'clock affair back at the lodge.

We'd poke into crevices, side channels, birds' nests; wander through spruce bogs, fir thickets, dead-end channels. Hope and faith dovetail curiosity like sound carpentry. Faith in what's ahead. Hope that it will be better than what's here.

A soft snore escapes his lips, and I get up and add another log to the fire. We fished the "hellhole" streams in northern Wisconsin and the Upper Peninsula of Michigan when I was in high school, marveling over sacredly iridescent brook trout that came darting out from log shadows to reward a well-placed cast. Few military bootcamps require what we commonly put ourselves through for a panful of fish. But the meals were another mark of solidarity, and harvesting my own food has ever since been important, as is companionship around a fire at night.

In 1969 I moved to Montana, technically for college, but actually to fish better water than Wisconsin and Michigan offered. My dad drove me out. We spent a week in Yellowstone catching trout on the Gibbon, the Firehole, and the Yellowstone, fabled rivers all, then drove on to Missoula. As soon as the perfunctory registration was accomplished, we headed up Rock Creek, where we caught huge brown trout on spinners held in the current and twitched. We had three of them cooked up at the Rock Creek Lodge that night for dinner, and I thought I was in heaven. I said good-bye to my dad, and hello to a fellow I'd met on the creek that afternoon, a fellow who lived in my dorm and taught me how to fly-fish.

Looking at my father now, I see a dusky creek, watch four salmon sweep the tail of the pool. See clear water, cloudy water, crooked water, flat water, calm water. The adventure of life I've been released into is both dramatic and tortuous, full of heartache and joy that is unique, universal, and at times mundane. But what keeps me balanced is the fact of rivers—that they exist if for no other reason than to be wandered. And this too was my father's gift, a desire to wander rivers. In their rhythms and seasons they teach me much of what I need, or want, to know about life. I raise a glass of cabernet to rivers and streams and creeks without end. My father sleeps on.

Once, in learning that things are not always what they seem, I stepped into gin-clear water that belied the fact it was over my head. Another lesson, that water was to be taken seriously, came when Blackfoot River bushwhacked me at the knees, knocking me forty yards downstream before I crawled coughing onto a gravel bar. But these were among the painful lessons. Others were the clarity of unimaginable cobble—mauve, rose, beige, and a rainbow trout hovering just above it, or the pointillistic beauty of riparian cottonwoods buttery gold in autumn light; or an eagle in Alaska sweeping downstream so close over our heads we could hear wind whistle through its feathers. And possibility around every bend.

Many times when life seemed to fill my foolish young heart with a pain so absolutely huge I could barely go on, I turned to and wandered rivers, and they nourished me. It took three cases of giardiasis to stop me from dipping my hand in and drinking the pure waters of Montana. And though I often wandered alone, I felt my father with me.

I remember his absolute patience when it came to teaching me how to fish. He'd spend twenty minutes untangling a backlash that would duplicate itself on my next cast. He'd usually lend me his outfit when my reel ran dry of line. Yet he seldom angered, and seemed far happier when I caught fish than when he did. We'd leave for Wisconsin, or Illinois's Chain of Lakes, before sunrise, running red lights at 5 A.M. (another lesson learned—a healthy dose of anarchy), and return after dark with a mess of bass, bluegill, pike, or crappie. My mother would always get up and share our enthusiasm; then I'd trudge off to bed leaving the cleaning and scaling to him. He taught responsibility gradually.

A succession of rivers and streams flow through my life as I watch him sleep: milky water of the Apple River that undercuts limestone cliffs where smallmouths hit drifted nightcrawlers; a gin-clear spring creek where fat rainbows hide in strands of myriophylum and suck tiny dun emergers; a river that curls away into moonlight and huge browns hit fast-stripped muddlers like southbound freights; an irrigation ditch chock-full of fat native cutthroats hungry for deerhair hoppers; a river alone under the firs, where chilling wind burns through our sweaters and we never see a fish, but a sole star shines in the translucent dawn sky; and a river that runs into sky through a valley as high and open as a cradle, where we catch over a hundred brookies a day. All these rivers exist simultaneously somewhere outside of time. And I hope he dreams these rivers and others as his head rests on his chest, which rises slowly and drops with exhalation.

He looks so vulnerable. I remember the first time our roles reversed. We were backpacking up the South Fork of the Sun River toward the Chinese Wall in the Bob Marshall Wilderness of Montana. The weather kicked up and a hoary wind moved in from the northeast. The trail, which had been rolling over the gullies and aspen-furred ridges, took a bend to climb for the sky, which roiled with bruised clouds. Eventually it broke out along a cliff face several hundred feet above the river, and after a hundred feet or so veered directly into a thirty-five-mile-an-hour wind.

My father has acrophobia. He's always had it, but it's become more pronounced as he's aged. He was ahead of me when he stopped. When I came up to him he was tipped and hanging onto the rock face at an awkward angle—the precarious leaning into a slope that seems intuitive but is exactly opposite of what one should do. I could see him shaking with fear. I asked him if he was all right, but my words were torn up by wind. We were in a landscape transformed from sunny glades and panoramic vistas to furious skies and utterly indifferent distance. We were pitifully small. We could die here and this place would not care.

I yelled louder. He turned to look at me but refused to give up his futile grip and move either ahead or back. I came up behind him and saw he was rigid. Sweat stood out on his forehead despite the wind. I didn't know how far the cliff trail went on, but our entire trip lay ahead of us. I edged past him, close enough to see I was hovering on another edge as well. As soon as I passed him I offered my hand.

"Come on. It can't be much further."

I could see his mouth move but again heard nothing but the roar of wind. Rain began to spit from a sky that seemed to descend on us. He took my hand. We moved painfully, slowly, inching along. He was either staring at the cliff wall to his left, or had his eyes closed. The trail finally curved out of the wind, widened, and left the cliff face, dipping into a copse of aspen. As soon as we were harbored, we dropped our packs and sat on a log in the meager shelter, rain soaking us.

I think we were both acutely aware of what had just taken place. A reversal of roles. I was now the father and he the child holding my hand. And as suddenly as the weather had turned, it turned back. The wind calmed, sun filtered into the thicket, and we saw steam rise from the cinnamon-tinted trail ahead.

One day after my father left for his home back east, I drove up the North Fork of the Nooksack River to photograph bald eagles, the hundreds that migrate here to feed on spawned-out chum and king salmon. I set off across the river bottom where it braids into as many as ten channels through the cobble bars, piling deadfall into heaps bigger than houses after each flood. Eagles were everywhere, hopping around feeding on chum carcasses, resting in cottonwood and firs at the river's edge. They fought and shrieked and chased off seagulls and crows. I worked on re-learning the settings of my old Pentax and dealt with the frustrations of a shutter that froze up in the seventeen-degree temperature.

Walking back to the car, I began photographing chum salmon on their redds. I became fascinated by one spawned-out loner, holding stationary in about eight inches of water, dorsal fin extruding like a sail above the surface. Its body was brutally attenuated by the fifty-mile migration and the denouement of procreation. A rash of fungus blotched its arm-long body; its jaw was a hooked and toothy weapon.

And what many thought ugly, I found beautiful and noble, and at the risk of anthropomorphizing, I imagined the beast in a final act of contemplation before moving on to the next realm. Even as I walked around it, it never moved, other than to feather its gills with serene regularity. Above me an eagle screamed, light faded, and on the river the drama of death and life continued.

A central truth of nature and the great religions is death. Shakyamuni Buddha is reputed to have said: "I am of the nature to grow old and die. There is no escape from this." His message is to treat every moment as if it is precious, your last.

I like to think that those of us who have spent many years fishing and hunting, walking rivers and woods, witnessing the cycles of seasons, of nature, of death and rebirth, are attuned to these phenomena. Rather than becoming indifferent, most of us become reverent. What we take away is also taken from us; what we give back and pass on is also given back and passed on. My father and I may fish together for several years to come, but that will not change the certainty of what we both face. I see him and that salmon resting side by side in a limpid pool, waiting, reflecting, gaining enough strength to face what lies ahead.

What my father gave me, and continues to give, and what I hope I pass on, I know best when I walk a river, as I did again today, and heard the scream of an osprey, the language of ripple and pool, and the hidden mysteries of quickness and depth. I feel him at my side when I glimpse a quicksilver flash in a dark pool or hear the pre-language of water over rocks. I feel him like a quick and vital urgency at the end of my line, as I move, as my father moves, around the next bend.

Dance of the Fathers

Each night I dream, and each morning I forget. It has always been this way. Sometimes a tiny fragment of dream stays on, its edges sharp, its colors vivid.

This is what happened, six months, a year ago: I was traveling in a country very far from here. I did not speak the language there, and the color of my skin and my manner of dress announced me as an outsider, a short-timer, one who would soon return home to another world. In that place the sunlight is harsh; little villages rise from thinly treed plains and cling tightly to sandstone cliffs along the escarpments. The villages are densely packed and chaotic, folding back upon themselves again and again. A fine, red dust fills the air, coating pathways, trees, and lungs; sometimes it thickens, carried by seasonal winds off the endless deserts of the north, flattening the light and obscuring the sun. The people who live there wrap themselves tightly against the dust and the heat, and they carry on with their lives.

The buildings are the colors of earth, stone, and dust. Mud and straw are mixed in shallow pits, patted into blocks, and left to dry in desert sun. The blocks are stacked into walls—thick at the base, then tapering with increased height—and plastered over with more mud. Woven branches span the tops of the walls, and these too are covered with layers of mud for floors and roofs. Each year the rains come, and after the rains the buildings are plastered anew; the mud is carried in cupped hands, pushed into place without tools, smoothed and rounded by flat palm and gently curved fingers.

Each night came dreams; every morning came forgetting, as always. After a time I left the desert, arriving soon in the capital city on my way to the seacoast. I rented a tiny room for the night, and in that room I dreamt I met a girl, ten or eleven years old, lean and tense. She had long red hair and startling green eyes, but when I looked in her face her skin was old and when I looked again her eyes were white, blind and turned inward. I dreamed that I spoke kindly, that with fingertip touch I gave her my blessing. At this she cried, and I held her, stroked her forehead and spoke softly.

And then came my alarm, shrill and insistent. I tried to hold onto the dream but lost my grip, got up unwillingly to leave that strange city in that foreign land where I could never belong and would not remain. The girl was then gone, the girl with the aged face and the vision turned inward. On my bus I looked away from the other passengers, and out the windows I watched little villages of mud and dust drift by, colors washing out in the heat. My throat thickened and the girl became somehow myself, still waiting, tense and unseeing, for the one who will bless me, for the one who will know.

I create my father each time I think of him. I invent a life of woven twigs, of straw and mud, and to it I plaster raw emotion, laughter, weariness, hints of wisdom. (Stiffly stands this thing, and immobile: hardly a life, surrounded by clots of spiky mud and tattered remnants of dried grass and branches.) This is my father, I tell myself, and I believe it true, and I describe him this way. But none of it is real; my father does not exist, has no form of his own, has accepted no form in all the years of his life. Still I try: still I mix straw with mud, I shape and I form, I patch the cracks when it shrinks and dries, crumbles to the touch, dissolves in the rain. My father, turned to grit, blows on the wind and coats the sills of distant opened windows, clouds the surfaces of still ponds in old fields now going back to forest. My father, grown old alone, weighs nothing: a thin, dusty film obscuring the surface of things between cleanings, between summer showers. A smudge, a blur, hardly consequential.

In my father's room the edges of things were hard and straight, and as a child I liked to sneak in to explore those sharp edges with soft fingertips. There was little enough inside: just a bed, a dresser, a tiny nightstand in matching bleached veneer, a few gloomy woodcuts hung widely spaced. His bed was narrow and square to the wall, and a single pillow sat at one end. There was nothing but space and sharp light, the sound of my footsteps rebounding directly off hard surfaces. I thought nothing of this, because in my father's room I saw reflected my whole self, and all that I knew.

My father had grown very old before I looked again into his room and—touching those same few hard edges—saw at last how stark and uninviting it was. There was no place to sit leaning comfortably, no place to relax reading, no place to put down a wineglass. My father has grown old now, his children terrible and distant; they do not think of him often. I carry my father's room with me wherever I go, as he carried it for his own father, but when I die that room will die with me. Outside are endless, empty corridors lined with locked doors. I hear echoes of shuffling feet, dogs whining, and a thin, faraway keening; the air is stale and difficult to breathe.

I inhabit my past, and I try to fill it with what is substantive. I am afraid of the empty rooms, the long echoing hallways, and I create my father now with an edge of worry, a kind of desperation.

It was my father who first took us camping, my sisters and I: my father whose Bronx-born delight in the wild places of the world first awakened my own. For one week each year we walked the hills and ancient mountain remnants of New England; at night we slept in leaky, waxed-cotton tents, swaddled in huge cotton sleeping bags, burrowing deep to escape the mosquitoes. When they got older my sisters stopped going, tired of the dirt and discomfort. I carried on, year upon year.

There are a variety of ways of approaching this telling, of course. Where do small children learn meaning, significance, value? Our family was uncommunicative at best, and I spent endless hours searching every detail of the world around me, tirelessly looking for something I could hardly have defined in the physical objects there. My father's photographs—gray air boiling crazy and harsh around piles of heaped and weathered stone—spoke eloquently of the importance of the wild places, the mountains. The photographs were black and white, but in my memory I see them in color—big, broad slumbering shapes dropping steeply off ridges into eroded glacial bowls—and the color is subtle, of lichen and krummholz in thick, swirling mists.

My father's way was to focus on the details, the small things. He would name them, and describe to me their functions and relations— the tree is a shagbark hickory and the rock, Precambrian granite; the cloud, cumulonimbus. My way was different: whole landscapes and their component parts became metaphors for myself and my life. Game trails wound and intertwined, appearing and vanishing unpredictably; dark clouds bore the threat of rain, snow, wind, storm; I found cliffs and holes, bogs and thickets; I imagined whole lives—entire worlds— that were lived in kingdoms of clouds. I became fascinated with maps, too: each sang me a narrative song of twists and turns, arduous river crossings, long thrashing journeys through thick brush, steep climbs to ridges connecting knife-edged peaks. Each told stories only I seemed to hear, of multiple lives lived fully, knit together, then ended. I studied the maps and the landscapes, hoping somehow to locate myself, to anchor myself securely in a world demonstrably unsafe.

"We'll take a trip out west," my father said again and again, "someday, when you're a little older." It seemed natural that he would pluck me from among the others; it would be just him and me, father and son, a road trip from mountain park to mountain park. He would like the same places that I would; I know this now because I remember his old photographs, and they show the places in which I have made my life ever since. But I knew it then also, and maybe this is the secret somehow: that his taste in landscape got into me early, lodged firmly in the same place that I carry certain turns of phrase, a way of holding my neck stiffly, a certain tone of voice when talking to children. Someday when you're older: a trip out west.

"When you're older" was of no use to me then, but I was a child, with a child's unforgiving thirst for whatever truths I could find and this one burrowed deep. When you're older, I heard him say, we'll drive west; when you're older you will become yourself, and I'll recognize you then (but not now) and in the wide spaces and mountain light of those old yellowed photos I will give you my blessing, and you will be my son at last. When you're older.

And then I was older, and he was gone. But I had a life of my own by then and could not have spent the necessary time in a car with my father, and could not have waited for him on the trails. I was sixteen; I fled to the West and discovered the Sierra Nevada in the late wintertime, all soaring sculpted rock and splendid high-country light, and there I made a home, my first. I presented myself to the world in elaborate strings of interwoven lies, hitchhiked back and forth and around the country, lived outdoors for months on end in groves of giant trees, in coastal chaparral with views of distant ocean, in leafy city graveyards, and under freeway bridges. I was sixteen years old, and I never went back to the world my parents had struggled to create for me.

I never went back. I carry that world even now, and I complain bitterly about its weight, but I never went back.

The years passed, and in their passing I became gradually myself. I worked, played, and lived mostly outside, and I discovered real wildernesses scattered across the continent, less tame by far than the places my father had taken me. One day, returning home from a trip in the far north, I detoured through those same New England mountains, driving gravel roads through an endless rolling sea of spruce bogs and low hills. I had come from more spectacular places, and I was unimpressed until I saw a range of hills that I recognized, somehow, from three decades before. They were broad at the base, rising steeply, then tapering gently to rounded, bare summits, one almost overlapping the next, huge and gray and still. In that massed volume, shifting between tension and repose, I saw a vast, slumbering strength. In an instant I became the small boy I once was, and the world outside my window roiled and was created fresh.

This was an older way of seeing: one which my child-self had known well but had quickly forgotten. As a young boy I found strength and safety in mountain landscapes—in the curve of rivers swollen with snowmelt, in the howl of banshee wind scraping bare New England ridgetops. Each summer I studied the road maps and views from the front seat of my father's car, searching the horizons for my first views of those rounded mountains where lay my strength. The fullness of my identification with those places allowed me to leave behind for safekeeping large parts of myself. I was wise and observant, and I chose carefully what I could not carry; it stayed safe, waiting for the time when I would remember.

Talking to my father now I hear something new, some hint of a grand narrative in the works. He is putting his life in order, hoping to tell what he has learned to willing listeners. . . . But there are no listeners, and the things he knows how to tell are not, at any rate, the point. My father carries stories deeply buried, of things he will never admit, even silently to himself. I see windowless basement rooms, chilled and gloomy damp, full of tapes spinning silently on old playback machines. There is no one to listen to the richness that is there, and no one to tell. My father, assembling his narrative, reaches for the fragments that will adhere disconnected memories to other isolated pieces, for the special integrating bits of history. In this place are the answers he so avidly seeks, and although he carries the only key, he will never enter here. I am the only one who knows that these basement rooms exist.

This, after all, is my special talent: to sense the gaps in the stories, to know when something is not being said. I learned to do this when I was very young. In the silence of my family, I was the one who knew the empty corridors, the basement rooms, the thousands of boxes there, all damp and musty, haphazardly piled; I know them still, even today. In those rooms I am what I was and will someday be; in those rooms, all time moves in parallel, merges and becomes the same, and the life of my father embraces my own, as mine embraces his. It is 1928, and he is waiting in the train station high above littered Bronx streets, the shouts of the pushcart men filtering up through timber and steel, the air cold and wet. He has been waiting for an hour, maybe longer, and the world is made of cotton and all feeling is muffled. His own father had promised to meet him here, but this man does not come and the cotton air muffles sound and numbs thought.

My father's father had no name, having left the family early, taken a new wife, begun fresh. There is another room, another time, and inside this room the nameless father of my father is dying, and this man he has not seen since those days waiting on train platforms is now gone. The news comes slowly, relayed through family. He is calm hearing this, and walks outside. I am in a tree, my favorite maple, overlooking our yard and the street, dreaming endless dreams that I promptly forget. Your grandfather is dead, he tells me, your grandfather whose name was never mentioned. I do not comment or ask questions ("But you told me he died long ago! What was his name?"). Instead, I file this information safely away, that I may take it out later and examine it for clues to the nature of the world. This is what I do with information. It does not occur to me to ask, and it does not occur to me to weep.

Now I weep. Now I know the grandfather I never met; now I carry him wherever I go. In another room I find my grandfather as he once was: sixty-five years old, a bald, wrinkled man. His arms are large, but his back is misshapen and oddly scarred, and his children are distant but he does not know this, having known nothing other. His heart will kill him soon, before he can begin to see the patterns in his life. (But he remembers, sometimes, an age before all this: the town where he was born in a distant country, another century, across the sea; his father was a cobbler and the winters were cold; a wrathful God battled servants of the devil there; the earth was alive, and it exhaled magic.) Has he heard of me, ever? Does he wonder sometimes about his grandson high in a maple tree, red buds leafing out in soft spring air? Does he ask about me, from time to time? At his feet are chunks of mud, drying slowly, and a sprinkling of straw.

My father carried with him the life of his father, a man he never knew. He gave this life to me in the form of certain images, a way of holding myself, an emotional reticence and a secret anger. It is difficult to see; others sometimes catch glimpses, but they do not know the starkness of my father's room, the swing of his shoulders, the way he absorbed punishment so, believing stoicism strength. They do not know the way he taught this also to me.

I can create him in any shape that I wish, so why this one in particular? Shall I tell instead another story? Look, then, at this man for whom familial strife is the worst of possibilities, to be avoided at all costs. He is a noble man, willing—no, let us say instead, eager—to absorb pain and suffer silently so that his children are spared the worst. He constructs his life carefully, deep in the background behind other lives, allows his estranged wife to raise his children, insists only on a single week with each child, far away, once a year. He takes us camping in the pine and spruce forests of northern New England; we hike broad, well-marked, graded trails, and he tells stories about ferocious weather, about losing the way and surviving terrible trials.

In this story I am nine years old, and I do not yet know my own vast anger. I love these north woods and the shattered granite of these ancient mountains because here there is room to turn my anger to energy. Here I can push hard uphill, easily outdistancing all others. I race the trains, I boot-ski loose rubbly stone in steep slide-paths, I range far, inspecting trees, stone, soil, streams. I do not know yet that I am searching for a dance, for that moment when I become weightless and unbounded, when I become wind and pure form in the absence of gravity.

I have always looked for this: racing the cog-driven train across endless fields of eroded granite; chasing wisps of wind across reaches of sand stretched to distant horizons. For me, there has always been this dance, and it is only now that I see that this must also be the dance of my father, though I have never seen any hint and he has never spoken a word. In the endless rooms where only I go, I am my father, and his father, and the father of his father. I am a middle-aged man trying desperately to leave behind the cotton air of the train station; I am eight years old, arriving frightened from a very different world across the sea; I am a shoemaker in a little feudal town peopled with magic and myth. I am trying to learn weightlessness and I am not done yet.

My father knows me best, of course. He does not realize this, does not understand, and I will not tell him. I can barely admit it to myself, and to tell would give away too much, leaving little; I have built a life around resisting my-father-in-me. What if I am devoured? What if I dissolve, fragment, turn to ash? (What if I am freed? What then? Start anew, build once again, learn to live with power?) No, I'll not tell him.

My father, who knows me well, granted himself no power, no substance. Instead he abdicated, lived deep in the shadows cast by those more vigorous, tried to fit the narrow spaces they left him, unobtrusive and inconsequential. I think that in his mind he took flight, lightly skipping and soaring, knowing air currents and clouds and the wild energies of the winds. . . . But he cannot say this, and I can see but will never tell. I know that he survived as best he could: tried to do what he thought right; told stories of transcendence on lonely mountain trails; lived alone, immobile and heavy, in a hard, bare room.

Who could have guessed that I'd wash up so broken, that I'd breathe shallow and nurse my wounds and study the clouds and learn, finally, to weep? That in the end I would become my father at last? I am my father, of twisted twig plastered with mud and straw, still soft and wet, formless and soluble, weighing nothing on the liquid surface of the world. I have no sons and I have no daughters: none to carry endless generations of cold, empty rooms, endless years of sadness never spoken. I do not offer my life for others to carry. With me dies my dance.

Father. Stand here with me. You never came so close, hardly existed at all except as I imagined you. But still you were my only guide, still you remain here beside me, and again now we are walking paths together that you never knew, remembering that which never could be. At our feet, weathered granite drops steeply to valleys, hidden in mist below. Color is muted, and the air is soft and friendly. Others have come this way before, and I see them just ahead, but there are none behind.

Others just ahead; none behind. I am carrying a blind girl with shining red hair and ancient, wrinkled skin, and she is sleeping now, calm.

Fishergirl

I am speeding across Nebraska on a train, on my way to Salt Lake City from St. Paul to meet my mother. We are going to travel the "Anasazi Circle," driving through Utah, Colorado, New Mexico, and Arizona to see the ruins of ancient pueblos—Hovenweep, Chaco Canyon, Canyon de Chelly, and Mesa Verde. Early in our planning my mother told me that my father would not be able to accompany us because he would not have time off. "You know," I said to her, "this is just for us. Me and you." She said she knew that from the start, but that she didn't want to put it that way to him. "Maybe you'll go on a trip like this with him someday," she said.

It saddens me that I can hardly imagine my father and me in a car together, traveling the West, staying in hotels, eating at roadside cafes, sharing small details of our lives. The only thing we have ever done together is fish. Fishing is the way we have known each other, and slenderly, silently, even then. When we fish, I am Fishergirl, still eighteen and living at home, and he is my fishing father. Beyond these stories we have written for ourselves, beyond these stories we have written for and on each other, the rest of who we are seems to fall tragically away.

There is a picture of me, taken by my brother Austin, in which I am dressed up as a fly fisher. I am eighteen years old, and I am on my first fly-fishing trip to Yellowstone National Park. I stand in the woods, a stream behind me, a pair of heavy waders strapped over each shoulder, baggy at the hips and waist. My plaid shirt sleeves are rolled up, my tanned arms bare to the elbow. My fishing vest is hung with gadgets. A piece of fleece on one shoulder is decorated with half a dozen flies. On my head is a gray felt hat, a goose feather in the band sticking out jauntily. Two long, blonde braids come down over my breasts. I am smiling, leaning slightly on one leg, my hands clasped in front of me. There is an innocence in my round, soft face. A look that says I am happy to be here, this is my place.

Years ago a college friend came to Salt Lake City to ski and to stay with us. My mother had placed the picture on a bookshelf in the living room. He looked at it, took it up in both hands to get a better view, and turning to me with a curious look in his face, as if he had only then realized something terribly important—he said, "It's you. This is you. It's perfect." For him, the picture stilled me, *dis*tilled me, represented me as I *really* am, as he saw me, as he wanted me to be. Fishergirl. It is a picture that I want to show friends, and a picture that I want to hide. When I look at it now, I feel like an imposter. Fishergirl. It is me, and it isn't me. It was me, and it wasn't me. It always has been me and never will be me.

It was my father who taught me how to fly-fish. And it was I who eagerly learned, never imagining that later, as a grown woman, the teaching would begin to feel like a molding. Never imagining that Fishergirl would grow to eclipse me, throwing a shadow over the many selves I wanted to become. I want to know, how much of me is this fishing girl and how much of that fishing girl is only borrowed, made up and put on? How much of Fishergirl is a sacrifice to my father's dream of a daughter, to my friends' desires for an eccentric companion, and how much is my own choice, my own desire? I want to let go of Fishergirl, shed her like a delicate snaky skin and start all over, making her up again, all by myself, as I go along.

On the train I lie with my head on a small, white pillow against the window, my curled body rocking, rocking with the rhythm of the moving cars. Even nested like this, I am restless. As always, I am disturbed by going home to the West, if not on the surface, then in the depths. It is only partly the severe landscape, the rocky dry March. I am agitated in the flesh-and-bone home of my body. The lost feeling started way back when the train left Chicago and is worse now. I get up and move through the train cars, descending to the lower level, furtively opening a window wide enough to feel fresh air on my face.

In transit, between one life and another, I forget who I am. I suffer again from an inexplicable loathing. "Let me out of this body," a voice inside me growls. My soul wants to take flight before we reach my destination. For a moment it is all I can do to stop from tearing myself limb from limb. In the train restroom, I wash my hands and face, lingering over my cheekbones as I dry them. "You," I say to myself in the mirror, "You are a pretty girl. Remember who you are." I look at my breasts, rounded under a rumpled blue T-shirt, my nipples showing through the thin cotton. I feel them being touched, gently by a woman

I love. I remember that I am loved. I remember that this is one of the beautiful and distinctive things about a woman, her breasts. Slowly, I come back into myself.

When I return to my seat I pull from my red backpack a book my friend Cate gave me, *The River Why* by David James Duncan. It is a book about fishing for people who don't fish. Such books abound. For Father's Day one year I sent my father a copy of Norman Maclean's *A River Runs Through It*. My father and I exchanged letters about the book. He liked it but was tired of books that pretended to be about fishing and were really about politics or love instead. Once he visited me in St. Paul and on my shelf found a copy of Richard Brautigan's *Trout Fishing in America*, a bawdy, political book about love and sex and fly-fishing; a commentary on the quality of life in America and how we treat nature. He looked through a couple of pages and said to me, almost angrily, "This isn't about fishing. This is crap."

I told him, "See, Trout Fishing in America is a guy, a man. It's a spoof on the myth and ideal of trout fishing." When Brautigan goes trout fishing he feels like a telephone repairman. He catches grotesque fish, not beautiful gleaming ones, but fish with ugly tumors and eyes half hanging out.

"It's supposed to be funny and ironic," I said again.

"I haven't seen anything funny yet," he said, shutting the book and putting Brautigan back on the shelf.

I open *The River Why* and start to read. Cate had given it to me nearly a year earlier, soon after we met. Inside the front cover she wrote in the lovely and difficult-to-decipher script that still amuses me, "Gretchen—about fishing and love and other matters of the heart—with great affection this Easter Day, 1993." We had known each other only a month. We had never been fishing together. We had only watched movies and talked, eaten at restaurants, browsed antique stores. She had never seen me with a fishing pole in my hand. She had never seen me in a pair of waders. On our first date I dressed in a black leather miniskirt and jacket. Underneath I wore black fishnet panty-hose and a white, nearly transparent tank top. My hair was freshly cut, clean on the back and sides and long enough on top to stand straight up. I waited for her on the sidewalk outside the restaurant, leaning with studied casualness against the brick of the building, my eyes shaded by sunglasses. When she arrived she daringly kissed me on the mouth in front of passing cars and couples strolling by.

After our date she gave me a note with a chocolate trout attached. 29

The note said, "For Gretchen T. Legler, Fishergirl." The chocolate trout was covered in gaudy, bright foil. The note went on: "You are such a work. So rugged and graceful and raw and polished and pure. You are like a river through me. Everything seems fluid and everything possible." Already to her, even then, despite my leather miniskirt, despite the shades, despite my urban *machisma*, I was Fishergirl. She too was imagining me this way from the very beginning. How is it, I want to know, that we become who we are in other people's minds, and exactly how true are their visions of us? Who invented Fishergirl, and why does she stay with me?

Cate loved one specific part of the book and had marked it for me— a poem by William Butler Yeats, "The Song of Wandering Aengus." The poem for me is about many things, but mostly about desire—the pursuit of a vision of oneself, the pursuit of the *possibility* of self, of joy. It goes like this:

> I went out to the hazel wood,
> Because a fire was in my head,
> And cut and peeled a hazel wand,
> And hooked a berry on a thread;
> And when white moths were on the wing,
> And moth-like stars were flickering out,
> I dropped the berry in the stream
> And caught a little silver trout.
>
> When I had laid it on the floor
> I went to blow the fire aflame,
> But something rustled on the floor,
> And some one called me by my name:
> It had become a glimmering girl
> With apple blossoms in her hair
> Who called me by my name and ran
> And faded through the brightening air.
>
> Though I am old with wandering
> Through hollow lands and hilly lands,
> I will find out where she has gone,
> And kiss her lips, and take her hands,
> And walk along long dappled grass,
> And pluck till time and times are done,
> The silver apples of the moon,
> The golden apples of the sun.

The River Why is about a fishing family made up of Mister Fly Fisherman himself, Henning Hale-Orviston; Ma, an inveterate bait angler, and their sons Gus and Bill Bob, both of whom suffer minor emotional problems and act out rebelliously as a result of their parents' constant dueling over the relative merits of bait and flies. Henning, you see, wants his son Gus to be a fly fisherman. Ma, on the other hand, wants her son to catch as many fish as possible on the crudest of baits. She is happiest when he catches a record bass on a rotten wiener. The book is not really about fishing at all, but a setting for a story about love and spirituality and finding your own way in life—finding a way that is your own, finding a path that is not any path anyone has expected for you, laid for you, or mapped for you. It is about finding out who you are. Who you are. Who you are. Who you are.

The train is making its way through a canyon along the Colorado River in Colorado. Hit now with late afternoon sun, the steep rocky walls are golden. As I try to read, I also listen to a family in the seats across from me. There is a little boy and a little girl. The parents are young and attractive. They laugh, they look each other in the eye, wink at each other, and consult often about what they should do or will do or just did with the kids. "Case and I are going to the potty," the father says, as they head off down the stairs hand in hand. The little girl is standing up on the seat looking out the window. The mother says, "It's pretty out there, isn't it, with the sun on the rocks?" The little girl says, "Yes, and the river is pretty, too." I look out and see a fly fisherman, knee-deep in the river, and a naked man, lolling in a tiny tub made with rocks to hold a steaming hot spring. Both the fly fisher and the bather are waving at us.

My mother is at the train station waiting for me, nervously scanning the train windows, watching the passengers getting off. But I make it across the platform and have her in my arms before she sees me. I am struck again by how small she feels, even wrapped in a sweater and parka against the late spring night. I am small, too, but feel beefy and huge compared to her.

It is well after midnight as we drive up from the valley and toward the mountains, toward Mount Olympus, at the base of which my parents' house nearly lies. In my mother's kitchen, around the table, the room lit by the white light of the stove top, we talk. We lean close to one another and whisper so as not to disturb my father, who was not up to greet me, but is sleeping in the basement in my brother's old

31

room. My mother reminds me not to flush the toilet upstairs because it will wake my father.

She tells me she has started doing something called container gardening. She points to two pots on the table, full of tiny plants. She is always starting something new, always following a new lead. She doesn't let herself get in a rut, become defined by the thing that she does. Once I finally got used to the idea of saying "My mother is a potter," she stopped making pots. Now she does container gardening, watches birds, and grows herbs and roses. She has finally grown a perfect rose, she tells me. So perfect, so deep red, so velvety was this Mr. Lincoln Rose, that she brought it to work to show it off. "It may never happen again," she says. "I had to show it to someone."

The day before we leave for our trip, my mother and I shop and pack. Not only are we shopping for ourselves, but my mother is trying to get the house in order for my father as well. She has gone to three grocery stores, all far away from one another, to purchase his favorite muffins, biodegradable toilet paper, and canned spaghetti with meat. She buys carrots and celery and cuts all the vegetables into thin strips and puts them in small Ziploc bags for his lunches. Then she makes lasagna for our dinner. During a normal week she will do all of this and spend eight hours a day working as a secretary. My mother's life makes me tired. She is sixty-three years old.

My father wants to spend time with me on this morning before we leave. First, he talks to me about his computer, his PowerBook, how it is the best computer he's ever bought and I should consider buying one, too. He then takes me on a tour of his new inventions. "Here," he says, "is my snow melter for the cabin." It is a big garbage can with a brass faucet pushed into the side. He opens the back of his truck to show me his new winch. He shows me his bicycles. I feel as if I am watching a kid open toys at Christmas. He asks me if I would like to ride to the store with him to get some glue. I say, "No, Mom and I have things to pack yet," and he turns away from me gloomily.

Between packing and shopping, I wander around my parents' house, as I always do when I am home, looking to see what is new and what is still the same as it always was. I open the door to my father's office. Once it really was an office, piled with paper and books, but long ago it was turned into a fly-tying and rod-building room. Now the room has an eerie abandoned feel, as if he got up one day and walked away from it, leaving all these artifacts behind. When my parents bought their land in Montana, my father stopped fishing so much. He stopped tying flies and became obsessed, instead, with building a cabin. His interests now are focused on composting toilets, solar power, battery banks, and wells. He is the first president of the landowners' association and spends much of his time mediating disputes between city slickers who, like him, bought thirty-acre parcels of the subdivided ranch their property is part of.

My mother warned me about the office. "I don't like to go in there," she said. "I think there may be black-widow spiders in the corners." When I open the door a rich and thick smell meets my nose—a smell of the skins of birds and old, old smoke. The walls are still thickly covered with plastic bags of fly-tying material hanging from hooks; peacock herl, rabbit fur, skins of mallards and wood ducks, tinsel and bright yarn, packages of turkey quills, pheasant necks, swatches of deer hair. The shelves are lined with tidy chests containing pullout boxes of hooks, bottles of glue, tweezers, and other small tools. Several fly-tying vises still are clamped to the edge of the desk. And from every surface sprout flies—elaborate streamers, tiny imitation mosquitoes, deer-hair grasshoppers of varying sizes, scrubby-looking nymphs, and elegant Royal Coachmans.

He had tried to teach me to tie flies. He gave me a book on fly tying for Christmas one year: *Jack Dennis' Western Trout Fly-Tying Manual.* Inside the cover it was inscribed "To Gretty from Daddy, Christmas 1986. I hope you will find this as useful as I did. You must still learn the basics first." I was twenty-six then. I never learned even the basics. The flies I did tie have all unraveled in my fly box.

That night around the dinner table it's mostly my father talking and me listening. My mother is quietly eating, sipping icy tonic water from a tall glass. She gets up and serves my father more lasagna when he asks for it. He talks about being close to retiring from his job as a professor and how university people are hovering, like vultures, waiting to move in on his space. He feels angry. He has worked hard and wants to be respected. It isn't fair, and I tell him so. In these rare moments when despite everything I see his fear, my heart opens to him. But it never stays open long enough to make anything change.

Still later, after we have spent some time talking about how I will be moving to Alaska soon, my father clears his throat and says, "I'd like to come up there and fish with you." A tiny, cramped part of my heart smirks. Fat chance, I think. I am moving to a new place, with a chance to start all over, a new life, and already he wants to come and fish with me. Already I am going there to be Fishergirl. What about the rest of it, I want to ask him. I am also going to Alaska to work, to start my first job as a professor of English and creative writing. I will be a teacher, like him. A writer. A member of a new community. I will be meeting people, dating, buying a home, maybe even building a log cabin. I will be so much more and other than Fishergirl. I want to smother my own desire to be Fishergirl and even suffer the damage I do to myself in the process, all to finally wreck this rickety bridge that joins us, to wipe away this part of me that feels so made by him.

We started out fishing as a family, my two brothers, my sister and I, my mother and my father. At first we fished from a small aluminum boat at big artificial lakes around Salt Lake—Strawberry Reservoir, Deer Creek. We fished for trout and perch, trolling big red and white lures. Or we fished from shore with worms and corn. We made jigs in the basement, pouring hot lead into tiny molds, then dressing up the jigs with black and yellow feathers. In the beginning we had trout in the freezer. We had trout for breakfast. We had trout in the sink, still wet and gleaming, just taken off the stringer. For years we fished this way.

Then things began to change, and we didn't have so much fish around anymore. Fishing became more about art than food. Both of my parents became interested in fly-fishing. It was my mother who started tying flies, ordering great quantities of feathers and thread and vises and scissors and glue from *Herter's* catalog. At first we still used spinning reels, attaching the flies to lines rigged with water-filled clear bubbles so that we could cast them far into the mountain lakes we backpacked to.

Fishing in our family gradually became more and more specialized, until tying flies and building rods became my father's hobby. My father took a special interest in teaching me to fly-fish. For me, as a teenager, it was something romantic and different. I made a transition, a leap into a new identity, that summer at Yellowstone, the summer my brother took the picture of me—I changed from a silly, ordinary girl with no boyfriends and straight A's on my report card into Fishergirl. The fishing will never be as good for me as it was that summer. My father would walk with me to the stream edge, pointing to pools where he said he knew there were fish. He showed me how to cast, keeping my fly line up in the air, throwing out enough line to get my fly to the shaded, cool bank on the opposite side. Then he would leave me to fish alone.

I caught cutthroat after cutthroat, moving slowly down the stream, fishing the big pools and the noisy shallow riffles, too. Sun warmed the back of my neck, the air was dense with the sound of snapping grasshoppers and the smell of sage and pine, all mixed with the coolness rising from the stream. Nothing then could have done me any harm. When I'd caught so many fish that my imitation grasshopper was frayed, I changed to something colorful and big. I didn't know the names, and I wasn't picky. I'd cast the fly upstream and watch its big wings float quickly down, my body tensed for the sight of a swirl, the popping sound of a trout's lips pulling my fly down into the water. Once, a voice startled me, "You're a natural, you know," and I turned around to find my father sitting on the gravel, his back against the cutbank, smoking a cigarette and watching me. "Do you like this?" he asked me then. I told him there was no place else in the world I would rather be.

The morning my mother and I finally leave for our road trip, my father is sitting in the kitchen with his portable computer and Post-it notes and pens of different colors. He props the computer up next to his cereal bowl and works. My mother reminds me he needs to be where it is light and cheery. He needs the sun, she says, or he gets depressed. But it means there is no room for her. She finally told him, she says, not to put his stuff out on weekend mornings when she is home. He does it anyway, and when she comes in he says, "Do you want me to move now?"

We tell him we're going to leave at seven in the morning. "Maybe you will, maybe you won't," he says crossly. I am finishing my last cup of coffee before we get in the car. My father and I are standing at the kitchen window, looking out at their cat, Bilbo, who is sitting awkwardly, one arthritic leg sticking out at a right angle, in a shaft of dusty sunshine on the balcony.

He asks me if I know how old Bilbo is. I say no, I can't remember when we got her. He looks me in the eye and says soberly, "Bilbo is twenty years old." I am appropriately amazed.

"She doesn't do much anymore," he says. "She likes to sit in the sun and sleep mostly. She's slowing down." He seems saddened by this, but also comforted, as if the cat is doing just exactly what an old cat, or an old person, should be doing—slowing down, enjoying what he or she loves best. The conversation makes me wonder about my father, about my mother, about how much time I have left with my parents. I guess twenty years, maybe. That's only a handful. I can imagine these years with my mother, but no clear picture of the woman I am now comes to me with my father in it.

I became my father's fishing pal. Some mornings I would be awakened so early that I cried as I tied my bootlaces, not wanting to go on yet another fishing trip, not wanting to go out into the cold morning. But later, on the water, as we motored through thick fog, and when I brought home a twenty-inch rainbow trout with a story about how it grabbed my red and white Daredevil when the lure had just hit the water, I felt sure that this was who I was. Fishergirl. When I was older we would go on Sunday trips, sometimes with my brother Austin, but many times alone. We would drive up out of Salt Lake, past Park City, into the mountains to fish shallow, rocky streams.

Somehow we became locked into a vision of one another as Fishergirl and her dad. I knew hardly anything else about him except this. For Father's Day I would send him wood duck skins, or trout napkins, or mugs with fish for handles. For Christmas he gave me boxes of leader material, little leather envelopes with sheep fleece linings for storing flies, small scissors attached to retractable cords for clipping fly line while standing up to your waist in water. One Christmas I opened package after package of fly-fishing gadgets. There was a zippered leather envelope full of half a dozen dazzling streamers, a brooch made out of a huge and elaborate fly, a mobile of a trout and flies, a little pad of fly-line cleaner, a spool of fly line. Mary, my brother's girlfriend, handed me another package, this one wrapped in lavender and tied with a turquoise bow. She winked at me. "This is for you, Gretty, because you're a woman, too." Inside the box was a bar of scented soap, body powder, and bath oil. Mary winked at me again, as if to say, he sometimes forgets.

When my mother and I leave exactly at seven, my father is in the shower where he can't possibly say good-bye. He went in there as we were heading out the door. I want him to be different. I want him to help us carry out our bags, to help load them into the car, to hug us each good-bye and kiss us on the cheek, to wish us good luck and good fun and to stand in the driveway and wave as we drive off into the morning. This may never happen. I can't depend on his changing.

Five hours later, my mother and I arrive at Hovenweep, our first stop. We walk down into a shaded valley, perfumed with sand dust and sage. The bluffs above the valley are ringed with dilapidated sandstone houses, put together brick by brick centuries ago. My mother needs to stop often. Her doctors won't treat her cough, she says, with some amount of anger. They just tell her to quit smoking. This walking is hard on her, but we go at her pace and I am in no hurry. We spend our first night at a hotel owned by a German woman and her husband in Cortez, Colorado. We get a message at the desk that someone has called for us. It was my father. We left an explicit itinerary with phone numbers so he knows exactly where we are. My mother calls home, and my father wants to know where the cat food is for Bilbo.

On the second day we go to the Four Corners and take goofy pictures. In one I am doing a Twister pose with my hands and feet in all four states and my mother's shadow is cast across me. At the Four Corners we both buy jewelry. My mother is gracious and kind to the Navajo women artists. She made pots for so long, and for so long sold them for not even half of the work she put into them. She knows how hard this kind of work is. "I love your work," she tells the women, and she smiles.

Before we go to Mesa Verde we visit the Anasazi Heritage Center. As we walk around the center, my mother coughs. I go from exhibit to exhibit looking at baskets under glass, a whole pithouse reassembled, panoramas, diagrams, collections of arrowheads, and artists' reconstructions of pueblo life. As I walk I hear her cough echo through the museum.

At Mesa Verde, we walk down to Spruce House. We are guided by a ranger who doesn't lie to us. He reminds me of Burl Ives—he has red hair and a red beard, a big belly, and a deep, friendly voice. His story about the ancient people is full of holes. "We really don't know exactly why they built in this canyon," he says. "Some people say for protection against marauding enemies. But you know, that's a particular idea that may be more about us than about them. These are only educated guesses." He asks us to speculate about the tiny houses built up in the thin wedges in the cliff. "Privacy," someone says. "Lookouts," someone else says. He smiles and suggests that in such close quarters maybe lovers used these huts as places to be together. This idea appeals to me.

At the visitors center I buy a book called *Our Trip to Mesa Verde, 1922*, a chronicle of four girls' trip to Mesa Verde in 1922. The girls, who were friends and schoolteachers, hiked the whole way from Ouray,

Colorado, to Mesa Verde and back, to see the cliff houses that were just then being excavated and opened to the public. Ruth E., Ruth H., Dot, and Fetzie were their names. How unordinary they must have been, four girls alone, hiking through the sage, in 1922. I envy them their bravery. I want to be like that. In the pictures they look wonderful and flamboyant in tall lace-up boots and dusty trousers, floppy hats, and old-fashioned packs. The trip took them a month. In the epilogue, written in 1988, Ruth E. writes that each one of them married and they all lived happily ever after.

At the hotel in Durango, Colorado, we joke with the two young women who are behind the desk. They are tanned and clear-faced with perfect teeth and wide mouths. Their eyes are bright. My mother asks if there have been any phone calls for us. I joke that we're on the run. "Thelma and Louise," my mother says, smiling at them and winking. The girls laugh. For dinner we eat at an Italian restaurant. For dessert my mother has custard with raspberry cordial sauce and wants the recipe from the waiter. She vows when we get home she will buy a cookbook to reproduce this dessert.

While we are getting ready for bed, my mother tells me that her arthritis is so bad now she can hardly pull on her pantyhose anymore. But, she says wryly, "The good thing about getting old is learning to accept yourself." I keep seeing her in a picture from long ago when she used to be a model. In the picture she wears a black short skirt, waist jacket, and pillbox hat. For a time, when we were young, my mother tried to teach Ally and me how to be ladies. She bought us each a pair of white gloves. She taught us how to roll on pantyhose. "Always wear your gloves when you put on your hose," she said, "or you'll put runs in them." Ally and I walked around the living room with books balanced on our heads, practicing good posture. She wanted me to learn to walk with my feet straight, not sticking out to the sides like a duck. She showed us how to turn, like models on a fashion show runway.

Most weekends when I was young, we went fishing. We would drive through mountain valleys, and at every bridge or roadside rest my father would get out and look at the water. Mostly we were all bored silly, fidgeting in the back seat of the car. But there was also a part of me that paid attention when he would stop the car on the side of the road, walk over to the streamside or look down on it from the bridge, and come back with a report. "Seems high," he'd say. At the next one he'd stop the car, get out, come back, "Seems muddy," he'd say. And again, "Looks clear."

This is one of the reasons I signed on as Fishergirl in the first place. I wanted to be like this—to be interested in and knowledgeable about one thing. His love of streams, of fishing, seemed so complete and pure and mysterious. He knew something we didn't, and I wanted to know what it was. I wanted to learn how to find fish, how to tell a good stream from a bad one, how not to frighten a trout in the water, what fly to use. Mostly I wanted to know what it was that he loved so much. I wanted to experience that, too, to love something so utterly you assumed everyone else was as fascinated with it as you.

I took my fly rods with me to college. I had two, both safely traveling in black plastic tubes, with my name on them in gold tape. Gretchen T. Legler. My father had made both of the rods for me and the carrying tubes. I stored the rods in my dorm room, in the back of the closet. No one I knew at college wanted to fish. But they all liked the idea that I had fly rods in the back of my closet. It made me interesting. A professor of mine flattered me by giving me a fly-tying kit—a big metal box filled with clear plastic drawers. In each drawer was something new—hooks of different sizes, colored thread and tinsel, feathers, hair, yarn, and glue. He had bought it thinking he'd get into fly-fishing, he said. But he had never opened it. I have moved the kit around with me to six different homes and apartments. I've never used it either.

One weekend in college I could not bear the city a moment longer and headed off to the rolling green hills of southern Minnesota to fish. I did some research and got the trout stream maps from the Minnesota Department of Natural Resources. I thought I knew exactly where I was going. As I drove along the dirt roads in the hot and heavy humid air, I slowly passed a black Amish buggy. Two little boys in flat straw hats grinned and waved at me. Their father, driving, nodded as I passed them. I was proud and feeling independent, feeling like Fishergirl.

I drove around all day looking for the stream that looked just right—something wide and deep, like the streams in Utah and Wyoming. But these streams confused me. They were all thin and muddy and covered over by trees. How would you fish a stream like this? A kind of indecision had seized me. I realized that this was no fun at all. The whole activity lost its meaning. I drove back to the city, to my dorm room and my books. I had not even wetted my line. I felt somehow stupid and false, as if I wasn't cut out for this at all, as if without my father by my side I was no Fishergirl at all. I wanted to be solid unto myself, and instead I felt full of holes.

When my mother and I leave Durango, we head off in the wrong direction. All the while we are driving happily and talking. We talk about her pottery. She tries to explain to me that the pots themselves were never her goal. That the whole thing was about process. And when she stopped making pots, it wasn't as if she had stopped being herself. She just moved on to something new.

Pottery defined her for me for so long. She was always in the garage working with a mound of clay on her wheel, loading her kiln, or in the kitchen with a pot on the table, rubbing the outside with a wooden spoon to make it shine. Her pots were mostly hand-built. She was trying, she said, to replicate Anasazi methods and designs. There was always clay on the doorknobs, clay on the phone.

Now she's stopped. She tells me that my father keeps asking her when she'll get back to pottery. "Maybe never," she tells him. She says to him, "I'm just not interested anymore." Now the garage is full of his tools and gadgets, and the kiln is on the back porch under a tarp. "What do you mean you're not interested anymore?" he asks her. She tells him that she is changing, that's it, and that he has changed, too; after all, he quit tying flies.

My mother and I get to Silverton before I realize we are going the wrong way. I tell her sheepishly that we need to turn around. She heads back up over the pass on the curving road we've just come down. It is cold on top of the pass. There is a lot of snow. It is beautiful. She tells me that she dreams about being on an endless road and coming to crevasse after crevasse and turning around. "This has something to do with life," she says, her eyes on the road, both hands on the wheel.

We talk about my being a lesbian. She tells me that since I told her this about myself she has discovered that everywhere she turns there is a lesbian or a gay man—an author, a friend, a movie star, and ordinary people, too. The letter I wrote to my parents, in which I revealed the reason I had left my husband, was boring and full of platitudes. It was full of short, declarative sentences. I had been careful with every word, every phrase. I wanted them both to understand plainly, with no flourishes, what had happened to me, how I had changed, how I had emerged. The letter had nothing in it of the joy I felt at the time. I was unaccustomed to the language of joy. The very word "joy" felt awkward in my hands. I had hardly a vocabulary to express myself, whereas

I had practiced for years the language of grief. "I am so happy," I told my parents in the letter. That is the word I repeated over and over and over. Happy. Happy. Happy. Only my mother understood. She turns to me now in the car and says, "You seem happier."

My mother telephoned as soon as she got my letter. I was sitting at the kitchen table by an open window. There was sun shining in. Cate sat next to me in a chair, holding my hand with both of hers. My mother did not say much. I had to chip loose what I wanted from her. I asked, "Are your surprised?"

"Yes and no."

"Are you sad?"

"Yes."

"Why?"

"The world is so unpredictable. Things hardly ever go anymore as you expect."

I was quiet.

"I have been thinking about how much it takes to raise a child," she said. "And I think we always did the right thing, but maybe not." She paused and then said, "I know we always did stop for ice cream."

Afterward, exhausted, I lay down in bed next to Cate and we slept. It had been easier than I had imagined, telling my mother. She had said all of the right things. "We still love you," she had said. But still, I was overcome by a deep weariness all mixed up with sadness and a clear sense of being suddenly released from a great, sagging weight. I was free. Free. Free of something. What? Free to do what? Be what? In my sleep I dreamed of my sister, Ally. I dreamed I was holding her hand, and I woke with Cate's hand in mine. I slept again, and awoke when I heard someone call me by my name. Still, Cate was sound asleep beside me. "Gretchen," the voice said, only once and very clear.

As my mother drives, I ask her why my father never called me about the letter. "I'll tell you, but you won't like it," she says. "He said he didn't care as long as you didn't tell everybody. He thinks sexual proclivities are private things."

"Oh," I say.

"And he never read your letter."

My heart lands like a stone in my chest.

"He worries about you," she tells me, "that it will be hard for you to be happy like this. That it will be hard for you to get a job." I laugh. My life has never been this easy. I have finally claimed space for myself against the forces that work to keep us all from knowing who we are; 41

the forces that keep us pasting ourselves together from the fragments of other people's desires. Of course, I think, he would never read my letter. He wouldn't understand it, and it would frighten him.

There is another picture of my fly-fishing. This time in color, taken by Craig when we were still married. In it I am wearing a bright red flannel shirt. On my head is the same old hat, adorned with a different feather—still long and gray, something I picked up along a stream or in the woods, vowing that I'd place it in my hat and never forget where it came from. My fly rod is tucked under one arm, and in my other hand I am holding a shining, flickering cutthroat trout upside down by the tail. I learned all this from my father. When you get the fish, you pull in line enough so you have the fish under control; then you pull your bandana from your vest, wet it, and taking the fish gently by its strong tail, lift it out of the water and carefully take the fly out of its mouth. Before you had even started to fish, you had clipped the barb off of the hook so that the fish's mouth would be hurt as little as possible. Then you let the fish go, first holding it by its tail in the stream until it has got its wits back and can swim away.

On the day this picture was taken, Craig caught an extraordinary fish. We had seen it lurking in the shade under the opposite bank, and Craig worked all morning to get it to strike. He played the fish too long, however, and by the time it was unhooked the fish was frail. And when he released it, the fish turned over on its back, its white belly open to the sky. Craig was cradling it in his palms in the water when my father appeared around the bend. He showed Craig how to resuscitate a fish by moving it slowly back and forth in the water, forcing oxygen into its gills. He did this with his big, intelligent hands until the fish flipped its tail and swam strongly upstream. Craig told me, jokingly, that he was lucky. He only caught fish when my father was there to see it. He seemed to understand so quickly something I had felt painfully all my life, that being good at fishing somehow wins my father's respect.

On one of our first dates, I took Craig to Hay Creek, a tiny trout stream in southern Minnesota. I wanted to impress Craig, so in preparation for the trip I called my father for advice. I told him that I didn't know how to fish these little Minnesota streams, and he told me I should use wet flies. Nymphs. He sent me a gift of a small packet of fluorescent green and orange "strike indicators," bits of colored foam tape you tear off and stick on your leader when you are using a nymph. You watch the strike indicator and when it stops moving, odds are your nymph is being nibbled by a trout. I hear his voice, "My nymph fishing improved about fifty percent when I started using strike indicators."

On that trip, Craig and I fished in ankle-deep water, catching two small trout; then we spread out a blanket beside the stream for our lunch. We played, putting grapes in each other's mouths, feeding each other sliced apples and cheese, and then started to kiss, finally making slow love in the tall grass. I saw sky over his back. I heard birds and the water. I smelled warm dust from the road. We washed naked in the cold stream, and I teased him that this was a risky idea he had had, what with the road so near. "It was your idea too," he said, smiling.

Craig took a picture of me on that trip that he later had a friend of ours make into a watercolor painting. I often think that it is only partly an image of me that emerged on that photographic paper; the rest is Craig's vision of me, fed by his love. The painting hung above our bed, until after we divorced and Craig gave it back to me—my shining face and blue, blue eyes, a green shirt, a green hat, and a yellow daisy in the hatband. In the painting, I look like a wood sprite. I look like Fishergirl.

My mother and I are winding our way toward Chaco Canyon on the third day of our trip. We take a thin, rutted dirt road, so narrow in places and hemmed in by red rock that I wonder if the car will fit through. It is early in the season and the road hasn't been graded yet. All the ruins here are in the canyon bottom, not up in the cliffs. Pueblo Bonito, the largest ruin in the canyon, is said to have been a mecca, a cultural and political center, crawling with people, surrounded by farms. There are roads carved in the sandstone, going up over the red rock sides of the canyon and leading to other pueblos. One story is that Pueblo Bonito got too large. There were a couple of bad years. Everyone died or moved. I want to know where the people went. I want to know what happened to their lives, their individual, private lives.

I tell my mother I am finally beginning to figure out my life. I am realizing that there are doors that will not always be open to me. I feel as if I am becoming wise, that my youth is ending. She looks at me and says quietly, "People talk about finding the meaning of life. People used to know what the meaning of life was—a job and a place to live and enough to eat. Life has gotten so complicated."

We talk about my father. She tells me that before my visit, my father asked especially for her to sit and talk to him about something important. They sat, one on each end of the kitchen table, and he told her that he was worried about my visit. He was worried that I would be difficult. Difficult. I would ask hard questions. I would rebel in small, insignificant ways. I would frustrate him by sleeping in late in the mornings, waking only after he had left the house, by staying up late, talking with my mother in the kitchen long after he had gone to bed, and by crying. "He always makes you cry," my mother has said on other visits. "I hope he doesn't make you cry. You don't have to let him make you cry."

My mother tells me that my father wants to spend time with me. "He wants to spend time with you *alone*," she says. "He tells me that he hasn't spent time with you alone in three years." Alone for what, I want to ask. Even when we are alone together, the space between us is like a vast canyon that our voices barely carry across. The last time we were alone together, we went fishing at my parents' cabin in Montana. We packed lunches and water and hiked down the steep slope to the Madison River. As we put on our wading gear and tied on flies, he talked to me about my mother. He said he loved her and didn't want her to die before he did.

"Have you told her that?" I asked.

"Not in so many words," he said. "There's no doubt in my mind. Unless I get hit by a car, I will outlive your mother."

He left me at the first pool. I watched him tromping downstream in his waders and fishing vest, his rod tip bobbing as he stepped over grassy hummocks, until he disappeared around the first big bend. I tied on a fly, something big with white wings that I could see easily in the fast water, and listlessly cast out and drew in line for two hours. My father, I knew, would be catching fish. He would be taking up netfuls of river water, scientifically determining the insects the fish were eating, and then finding (or tying) an exact match.

When he came back to join me at lunchtime, he found me lying in the sun, reading a mystery novel. Beside me I had a stack of reeds I had collected for my mother, who wanted them to thatch the roofs of the birdhouses my father had been building from hollowed-out logs. He set his rod down in the grass and took a sip of water. He asked me, "Have you ever thought we were rich?" I said no. "Well, we're not rich. We never have been. But Mother has done an incredible job managing our finances, so we have a good ratio of income to outflow and a good retirement." I asked if he had told her that. "Not in so many words," he said. "I'm tempted to ask her to show me how to do it. I'm going to need to know." I want to ask him with what words or what actions he *has* told her that he loves her. I want to ask him if he loves me.

On the fourth day my mother and I leave Gallup and go to Window Rock on the Navajo Reservation. We stop at the Hubbell Trading Post and visit a shop where Navajo women are weaving. My mother wants to talk to them, but they only smile at her. She looks at a young woman standing nearby and says to her, "I guess I don't speak their language. Can you ask them how long it takes them to weave one of these rugs?" The young woman says something to the older women, and then turns to my mother and says, "These are women in their seventies. They only speak Diné. They never went to school. They were old-fashioned and stayed home all of their lives, you know. It takes them hundreds of hours to weave a blanket." When we leave, my mother thanks the old weavers and the young woman who was her interpreter. My mother is one of the nicest people I know.

In the beginning I liked that fly-fishing with my father made me feel somehow superior to people who fished with spinning gear and bait. I felt as if I had evolved into a more refined and more intelligent creature when I learned to fly-fish. I would laugh at the jokes my father would make about hayseeds who fished with corn and cheese balls. But after a while the jokes didn't seem funny anymore. On one particular trip I remember feeling ashamed and putting the shame in my pocket like a shell or a tiny pinecone.

My father and brother and I had set out on an already hot, dry morning for the lower part of Slough Creek in Yellowstone. We had taken a shortcut over a steep hill, into the woods, where we often saw moose and deer. Far away, up higher on the green meadows, we had heard elk bugle. Along the way we met a horse-drawn wagon taking this route to a dude ranch north of the park. We got to the stream, and there was no one there yet. As we sat on a log by the very first pool, quiet at that time of day, still and amber-colored, we peeled off our boots and wool socks and put on waders and wading shoes and got our fly rods set. I was missing something, as always, and had to ask for it — some tippet, some leader, maybe a few extra flies. My father handed them over impatiently, as if to say, you're old enough now to have your fishing vest in order.

As we were preparing to fish, a father and son arrived, talking loudly, breaking the still. My father muttered under his voice as they moved away, walking merrily along the high grassy bank, that they would scare the fish, that they shouldn't be allowed here with their spinning gear and flashing, hook-heavy lures. I told him in the kind of controlled, angry voice in which I was learning to speak with him, "It isn't our stream." He looked at me and smiled and said, "Yes, it is." Instead of feeling fine and laughing, I just felt snobbish, and I knew it wasn't right.

We are headed to Canyon de Chelly. My mother describes a movie to me about a woman and a man who fall in love. He's an ex-con. The man and woman kiss in the movie. It is their first kiss, tentative and full of passion. She could feel the passion, she says, the electricity. She hasn't felt that way in a long time.

"Is that what you feel?" she asks me, tentatively.

"You mean with a woman?"

"Yes," she says.

"Yes," I answer. "Now more than ever before." I try to explain this to her. "It wasn't that I never had great sex with men," I say. "It's that with them, with men, I was never fully present in my own body." She tells me that she is surprised and a little embarrassed that I talk so easily about sex.

At Canyon de Chelly we walk down into the wash to see the White House Ruins. I keep handing my mother my water bottle and urging her to drink. "Water is good for you," I say. It is a steep walk, and she goes slowly. At the bottom there is thin spring grass and a hogan, and red walls rising up to blue cloudless sky. We walk along the wash in the deep sand to the ruins, where there are other people who have come down in four-wheel-drive vehicles with Navajo guides.

At the ruins some women have spread out blankets and are selling jewelry. I buy a silver medallion, shaped like the sun, on a leather string. Coming up from the bottom of the canyon, my mother takes a picture of me in my bluejeans and ribbed, sleeveless undershirt, the medallion around my neck. In the picture I imagine coming from this shot, I look hot and tanned. I am smiling. My breasts show rounded under my shirt. This will be a sexy picture. Cate will like this, I think. I have never felt this way about my body before—recognizing it as desirable. It is the same body I have always had, but I am different in it now.

The last stop my mother and I make is in Kayenta, Arizona. As we drive there, night is coming on and the clouds above us turn slowly from pink to peach to gold. The clouds are so close and the color so intense that I feel as if we are rising up into them, as if we are flying, as if at any moment we will burst through this blanket of gold and be soaring among stars in a blue-black sky. At the hotel we have Navajo fry bread and salad for dinner. Just to watch her order from a menu, to see her make a choice about what it is that she wants, such a simple choice, gives me a feeling of greater intimacy. Neither one of us sleeps well. Clearly, we don't want to go home.

As we drive through Monument Valley the next morning, the sun comes up deep burnt-orange behind the weird sandstone sculptures of the valley. My mother keeps saying to me that this is the best vacation she has ever had. "You're easy to be with," she says. She is surprised by the things I do for her, such as open doors and carry her suitcase. "You are so polite," she says.

When we get back to Salt Lake she wants to have our pictures developed right away. We drop them off at the camera counter at Safeway, even before we reach home, and rush back to get them exactly an hour later. We show them to my father. He looks at three or four and puts the stack aside.

There is another picture of me fly-fishing. I am older still. Maybe thirty. I stand in a wide, curving stream with my fly rod, casting out into the silver water with trees rising behind me and gray-blue mountains beyond that. The picture looks romantic and perfect: girl and stream. Mountains. Fish. But I remember this time. I remember my heavy pack, the blackflies biting at my neck, my Royal Humpy caught on the rocks and willows behind me. I remember not catching fish and wondering again why I was out there in the stream up to my thighs in water.

I remember, too, that there was then, and has been every time I have gone fishing with my father, a laughing in the water and the pleasant crunch of gravel under my boots and relief offered by the cool wafts of watery air that came up from the stream. There was the rich smell of fish and weeds and pebbles and muck from the undercut banks hung over with grass.

I remember, too, amid the peace and the real joy, a feeling of being trapped. I don't love this, I wanted to shout out so that my voice echoed off the mountains. I'll never love it like you do. Can't you see? I'm doing it for you, to be with you. I'm trying. And it isn't working.

My father agrees to take me to the train station at five in the morning, long before my train is supposed to leave. Already he had been up for hours, typing on his computer at the breakfast table. He will go straight from the train station to his lab and work. He asks me if I will come and visit him at his cabin in Montana this summer. I tell him no. I can't spend time with him alone now, until something, anything, even something small, changes between us. He asks me what I would like for my graduation present and suggests some stocks that his parents gave him when he graduated with his Ph.D. in biology. In the secret, angry language that passes between us, I hear him saying that he loves me. I want him to say it out loud. I want him, out loud, to ask me something real about my life and to tell me something real about his.

Our strongest connection lies in fly-fishing, but I want more than this—I want him to understand me in my wholeness. I want him to know what else there is about me besides Fishergirl. "You want me to fish with you," I want to say, "I want you to see who I am." And I want to tell him this, that I am an ordinary woman who is thirty-four years old and owns a stained, smelly fishing vest, only half of the pockets with anything in them at all. I am an ordinary woman with a crumpled and eclectic collection of flies, an unused fly-tying kit, two fly rods, two reels, some cracked nylon wading shoes, a pair of old-fashioned rubber waders, and a couple of books on fly tying. And besides all of this, I have two cats. I like to drink strong coffee in the morning. I dance the two-step to country music. I own a leather miniskirt and purple cowboy boots. I love my crewcut hair. I sip chamomile tea every night before bed. I have gone canoeing in the wilderness alone. I won a medal in a cross-country ski race. I have ordinary desires, to love and be loved in return. Bills to pay. I am moving to Alaska. And I am a lesbian. He has no idea of who I am.

He hugs me awkwardly, and when I look at him tears are pooling in his eyes. After he leaves I sit in the waiting area and open *The River Why* again. In the last chapters, Gus goes off to a cabin in the woods to fish and be alone. Released finally from the pressing of both of his strong-willed parents—the fly fisher and the bait angler—Gus finds himself, and he finds his true love, a glimmering fishing girl with apple blossoms in her hair. In many ways he gives up on his family, gives up about them ever being different, and sets off to have a new life.

One day, upon returning to his cabin, Gus sees, by the stream that runs in front of his house, an old man with a straw hat tipped over one eye, lounging in a chair and fishing with worms. He doesn't recognize the fellow and lets him be. Farther along the stream Gus sees an old woman elegantly decked out in tweeds, fly casting perfectly. He doesn't recognize her either, but watches her for a while, impressed. Soon he begins to realize that he does know these two. He realizes that they are his mother and father and that they have changed.

When the train arrives I shut my book and move out into the darkness of the platform. I shove my bags aboard and settle into my seat, my face pressed against the window. The train doesn't move for a long time, and I drift off to sleep, dreaming. In the dream my mother is in her kitchen. She wants me to spend more time with my father. "He has something important to show you," she says. My father enters the kitchen, pale and thin, with red and tired eyes, but he is excited, like a boy, showing me his latest miraculous inventions—a new way to fasten rain gutters to the cabin roof, or this, a clip for attaching a cable to a battery, or this, blueprints for a straw toolshed. As I turn away from him, he collapses, folding to the floor like a dropped cloth, and I run to him calling "Daddy, Daddy, Daddy."

I am startled awake by the train lurching away from the platform with a deep metallic creak and a moan. My heart is pumping unevenly in my chest. I whisper to myself, the words coming out softly and making misty spots on the window glass near my face, "Is it time?" Is it all right to go ahead and admit that I am blood of his blood, that I am my father's daughter, that *this*, that loving to fish, is a gift, that we love some of the same things? In a moment so bright and quick that I hardly know what it is, I understand one thing—no one can really do that to anyone else; no one can really fix or freeze anyone else. But it has been hard to contradict the molding. The more I know who I am, the more I will be able to see who I am. I smile to myself over how much of a riddle it sounds. I am, at least partly, and all on my own, Fishergirl.

As we begin to move, to gather speed, something begins to gather in me—it comes slowly, then faster, then comes on all at once, like a river of heat rolling up from my toes, filling the hollowness of my body, making my scalp prickle, my fingers tremble. This is joy, this thing I was so unaccustomed to not so long ago. *I have changed*. I close my eyes and see a glimmering girl emerge from a silver trout, lithe and shining, running, calling me by my name.

Recoveries

I never told my father this, but late one night, home from college, I nearly lost his car on the street in front of the house where he and my mother lived in Tacoma.

Beneath the front porch light, too late even for moths, I pushed the key into the lock pin by pin to disturb no one. Wobbly from the beer and cool dark morning hours, but prodded by something, maybe the fear of being seen, I looked back over my shoulder. As if trying to sneak away, my father's robin's-egg blue '62 Ford station wagon was rolling backward down Huson Drive and gaining speed.

In the sobriety of adrenaline, I caught the car twelve strides later. The tires chirped when I hit the brakes, but no other sound that late night—no lights on suddenly, no last cricket to accompany my heart thudding for the imagined crunch of fenders and quarter panels, and the tinkle of glass. I started the car again, reparked it, held the shift in park, and set the parking brake. Hadn't I done that?

My father may have been watching but never said. He was always watching, but sometimes could only shake his head at what he saw. At the fate of each of his new cars, for example. As if clean lines and new paint blinded her, my mother scraped their new '52 Mercury against a light standard. His new '55 Ford sedan my mother backed into the neighbor's car. His new '61 Ford station wagon I backed into a telephone pole late one night three days after I had earned my driver's license. He was asleep when I got home and I tossed and turned in bed, worrying about what I was going to say to him. The next morning the heel of my right hand was scraped raw, and I remembered a nightmare wrapping me in tentacles. But I didn't remember trying to pound my way through the bedroom door that opened inward, yelling, until my father finally shoved the door open, grabbed me by the shoulders, and shook. "OK," I said. "I'm home."

My mother was worried, she said on the phone. "Your father sits in the car in the driveway and won't come in." I was attending Washington

State University at the time, playing basketball for the Cougars three hundred miles across the state. I thought of my father's solitary side—the rock wall he built by himself in their backyard with a shovel and crowbar, for example. In the summer I'd find him late afternoons re-setting stones and whispering to no one. He wore black work pants and a T-shirt and a baseball hat and would stop to talk a moment.

"Can I help?" I'd ask. He'd say thanks, but no, and I'd climb back past all the asters and hydrangeas my mother had planted in the small plot of ground he worked for years to shore up.

It's as if he took it on himself to frame our lives and within those frames allow the spontaneous and wild. When I think back, I realize he always left something undone in his own life, something a little wild. When I was very young, we lived at the north end of Seattle in a small house on 171st Street. My father's first landscaping project was to build a river-rock wall around the front yard's madrone tree. But the ma-drone would not be contained.

I will never forget the litter of that tree, bark peeling, the leaves falling, a fecundity of trash that I was asked to rake up twice a week. The tree knew no seasons, no moderation, and dropped dinner-plate-sized indestructible pitch-coated leaves all over my father's new front lawn. Their disposal was my job along with the strips of bark and the tree's waxy red berries. It was worse than dishes or laundry. I hated the front yard.

However, the backyard had potential. Although my father built a cedar fence six feet high and planted his lawn and flower beds, he left one corner, maybe a quarter of the yard, unfinished. There he dumped peat moss and, one horrible summer, a pile of manure for my mother's flower gardens. The rest of the ground I laid claim to. I dug traps, more intrigued by the deadfall and the camouflage than by what I might catch. I started fires, set up tents, built a lean-to, dug in a home plate from which I drove baseballs that loosened the nails of his fence. He let me do all this. He even set up a regulation ten-foot basket that I couldn't reach for years.

The fence was the limit. At first I couldn't climb over it, but the older I got the easier it was to vault. Into Mr. Ruland's yard, past the neigh-bor's dog gone spastic with barking, and into the woods. My father had no intention, I believe, of enclosing anybody, but he wanted me to know that there were benevolent limits, where he made his presence known, where he stood, in effect.

After I could finally get the ball up to the rim, my father stood on the sidelines for years, watching me play basketball. When I played at Wilson High School in Tacoma, I remember asking him each morning for a ride home after practice, which ended each evening at 5:30. Invariably he was there at 5:00 and sometimes 4:30, standing in the doorway to watch. He attended all the games, though he said little afterward besides "good game" or nothing in sympathy if we lost. Once in a game against the Black Knights of Bremerton, the Navy kids from the other side of the Sound who played dirty, I grew tired of the pinching and the fist in the kidneys and the rooting out on rebounds, and threw an elbow that caught my opponent in the temple. It was a sucker punch I'd planned since halftime, and before the Black Knight stood back up, I had run down the court. After the game, which we won, my father seemed more silent than usual. Full of myself for the victory and for my assault, I asked if he had seen my well-placed elbow.

"I wish I hadn't," he replied, and then drove on in silence. It was what such mean behavior deserved—the threat of his absence. Devastated by that, I knew immediately how petty that elbow was, and worse, how inappropriate my crowing about it. The chill rode home with us.

All those years I was growing up, his teaching was an articulation of place—Sekiu and Neah Bay on the Strait of Juan de Fuca, Point No Point and Hat Island on Puget Sound, the Hoh River, La Push and the Quillayute River, Westport and Ilwaco on the Pacific Ocean. He wanted to fish, and he took me along. From Seattle, we would drive south through Olympia and then up through Humptulips and Queets into the Olympic Peninsula, the two-lane road a tunnel through trees where logging trucks roared. I remember once outside Forks, a load of cut and cleaned cedar logs, three feet in diameter at the butt ends, lay topsy-turvy beside the road. "Busted loose," my father said, and for miles I imagined every logging truck on every curve, tipping as we passed, air brakes growling, the chains snapping, and twenty tons of cedar logs rolling our car flat like pie dough.

"Look, look," he would say, and there would be deer or elk in a field, and one time in the narrow road of the rain forest, a cougar on the center stripe looked hard at us before it leapt into the green.

Sometimes we took a ferry across Puget Sound and Hood Canal and then drove north through Sequim and Port Angeles and up the road past the one tavern and gas pump of Pysht, Washington—"Psst," he'd say every time, and then, "Too late, you missed it"—and finally, late into Sekiu where we parked next to Olson's boathouse, peed in the woods behind, and found bed springs leaning against the wall and an old smelly mattress to sleep on. In the corner behind kicker boats overturned and stacked, we would lay the mattress out and sweep it with the flashlight beam and brush away the mouse turds and unroll our sleeping bags. Lying there trying to sleep next to my father, I could smell the salt air and boathouse oil and listen to the foghorn and sometimes the clack and rumble of a late logging train rolling down from the forest into Sekiu to dump its logs into the Strait.

For a boy, it was all wonderful—the scrambled eggs, pancakes, and orange juice the next morning in Martha's Cafe, the bait shop with its Day-Glo panorama of lures, chrome flashers, and buckets of lead. From the trunk of our car, my father hauled his fifteen-horse Evinrude down to our rented, sixteen-foot kicker boat tied at the dock, then the gas can, frozen herring, a cooler of sandwiches, rain gear, life jackets, poles and tackle box, net, and compass for the front seat. Early we would push out into the Strait, everything we needed stowed in our boat. Beyond its gunwale beneath the great green rollers hid the salmon we had come so far for. My line disappeared into the swells. And up rose seals, and box jellyfish, and kelp, and schools of pilot fish, and once the black and white back of a killer whale rolling up not ten feet from our boat, the dorsal fin taller than me. There were gulls and ling cod and halibut, and every once in a while the tap tap at the line and then the pull and set, the winding, and a coho would work its way up until silver flashed in green water thirty feet from the boat and out it would leap like a trout, head shaking.

My father loved the self-contained rhythms of fishing, the ritual of an early start, the catch and the tending to it, and maybe most of all, the solitude. Once in La Push, he took me to commercial boat docks in the evening when the long liners motored up beside the dock to weigh their catch, fish by fish, in the broker's scale. Many of these one-man trollers didn't seem much bigger than our kicker boat, with a small cabin and outriggers above hand winches, and two-cylinder inboard diesels wheezing thump by thump at idle. My father said they'd store up on ice and stay out several days, and when they caught enough they'd come in over the bar and wait in line here.

The one fisherman I remember, bearded in oil slickers, reached into his hold to lay silver after silver salmon at the broker's feet, who weighed two or three at a time in the scales, bright fish five to eight pounds apiece. And when the fisherman stood straight up a moment as if to rest his back, the broker opened his book to write a check on the spot. "One more," that fisherman said, in the best of dramatic pauses, and reached down into the ice and lifted with effort a huge king onto the dock. It made up ten of those silvers, maybe fifty or sixty pounds, and deserved a scale all to itself. Strangers glanced at each other and took a breath, and the broker crumpled his first check and commenced to write another. I could see on my father's face that a small, self-contained fishing boat on the Pacific Ocean would suit him just fine. He told me years later when he was about to retire that he wanted to buy an Airstream and park it overlooking the Pacific at Westport. He thought he could get a job as a bait boy, anything to keep on the water. As it turned out, my mother had other plans.

"Shoot them all off before we go home," my father warned. I was born on the fourth of July, and at thirteen wasn't more than a short hormonal fuse away from exploding myself. That Fourth of July weekend, as our family was driving to Mukilteo, Washington, I was surprised when he stopped at a fireworks stand and said pick out something. Of course, I chose the six-dollar Racket Box. Not one pretty thing on the contents list. It had Black Cats and Thunder Bombs and M-80s and Lady Fingers and Yankee Boys and every assortment of noise from buzz to bang.

We were on our way to Hat Island, six nautical miles off Mukilteo and three miles around, and for one weekend and the island's entire circumference I held small wars with sea gulls, dented cans, blew up bunkers and driftwood houses, launched sand crabs, exploded kelp bulbs and stubborn clams, and lifted up geysers of water with cherry bombs. I stirred the outhouses, singed my fingernails, blew my hair back, and never in three days risked an aesthetic moment. The last act of my noise symphony was the mortar, maybe an eighth of a stick of TNT, to be shot straight up from its stand, the final salute. When I lit it and backed away that early evening, however, the wind blew it over, and down the boardwalk and under the cabin's porch my bomb skipped. Oh, how my mother and father and their friends, John and Helen, jumped, the flash and roar two feet beneath their wicker chairs. Bravo, bravo, I thought I heard someone say, but my hearing hadn't been right all weekend.

It was not the last time I would complicate the best-laid plans, mine or my father's. When I was courting Penny, now my wife, my father asked us if we would like to go charter fishing at Westport, one of my father's favorite activities. The ritual was as follows. Three-thirty A.M. departure from Tacoma, a stop at the Aberdeen café for breakfast and fish talk, either old stories retold or speculation about the day's possibilities, tides, and catch patterns, and the weather always. A license at the bait shop, the sky near blue. Then gathering on the dock before the charter boat—this time a small six-person boat—the dawn departure, crossing the bar at the mouth of Gray's Harbor, a dramatic ride on the incoming rollers, and then a ride out the buoy line.

I could see that despite her preparation with Dramamine, Penny looked pale and queasy down in the hold. "Don't stay in the cabin," I advised, trying to sound authoritative. After all, I had never been seasick in all the times with my father on the Sound or out here in the Pacific, and I took this as a point of pride.

When we finally motored far enough out, the captain cut the engine, and we placed ourselves around the boat, my father at his favorite spot in the bow. I showed Penny how to rig her line, explaining how the cut-plug herring impaled on two hooks spins to mimic a live fish, how many strips of line to let out, and what to do if a fish took the bait. I knew everything, stood beside her as resident authority, having done this with my father for years. Such is the odd mix of love, pride, and hubris, a kind of lure, of course, for cosmic irony.

For it allowed me to hook the first fish on the boat, even before I could light the cigarette I held in my lips. There was the strike, the tap tap, and I set the hooks. I felt blessed. A salmon running. "Fish on, fish on," I yelled and moved sideways along the rail as the fish ran out at an angle away from the boat. Line zipped out, my Penn reel spraying water. The rod jerk-jerked and then lightened up, and I reeled as fast as I could because the fish was running back toward the boat. No slack, I heard my father say in the back of my mind. Rod tip up. And then the fish turned again and I crab-walked against the rail toward the stern of the boat, which reared up at that moment on a wave. As the salmon tore straight out, I leaned forward against the brass chain that guarded the only open spot in the boat railing, the two-foot-wide entrance we had stepped through onto the boat an hour before, the chain that held my kneecaps and my bravado, the chain I trusted.

Balance never seems precarious until you lose it. Then it's gone. Simple and certain. No decision, no analysis, no argument, not a single negotiation would have changed my falling headfirst in a great and slow-motion arc into the sea. My glasses unhinged from my face and tumbled away, but no matter. I was not going to lose my father's sacred fishing rod, and witnesses on the boat, befuddled for a moment by my amazing disappearance, testified they saw first a tip-top guide, then a rod rising out of the sea, a reel, my hand, and then my head popping up beside the boat. The first thing I saw was Penny looking down, no longer pale. "What should I do?" she asked.

"Take the rod, please," I said. "Take the rod."

Next to her, my father said, "Oh, Christ, what now?" and shaking his head, leaned down and grabbed my belt with one hand and my coat collar with the other. He was a big man, over six feet three inches tall and weighing 250, and though I am big enough in my own right and was waterlogged at that moment, it didn't seem to matter. My father winched me out of the sea and dropped his biggest catch of the day, dripping and puffing, onto the deck. It happened so fast the shirt beneath my coat stayed dry. I still had the filter of my cigarette, the tobacco and paper washed away, clamped in my lips. I looked around. The captain of our charter boat blabbed into his CB the news that would make me famous in Westport. Penny handed me the rod, and I lifted and wound the reel and found, to my surprise, the fish still hooked.

Years later I wrote a poem in which that fish escaped. I took Richard Hugo's advice and changed the triggering story so that "my salmon / [with] one last desperate leap / shakes the hook free." I'm glad I did. The historical truth, however, is that I caught the fish, and the next night back in Tacoma my father barbecued salmon fillets and my mother made potato salad and tartar sauce, and we drank toasts to good fishing and even better recoveries. The next day, the story was taking on a life of its own and would develop over a decade of salmon dinners as mildly heroic or sometimes cautionary but always comic. My father admired that I'd still caught the fish. Penny said she was afraid I might drown and forgot all about her seasickness. "Weren't you worried?" she asked my father.

"He can swim," he said without a fuss.

I was especially glad I hadn't lost his fishing gear, although I squinted hard until my next pair of glasses. Given her experience at sea, I was elated that Penny accepted my proposal of marriage. When we told my father over dinner one night, he toasted us and wrote the date and our names on the wine cork. It felt like a handing over, and the fact that corks float escaped none of us. By this time, my father fished less and less and spent more and more time trimming his yard and edging and turning stone after stone before his never-finished rock wall. Flowers bloomed all around his house, and the fir trees in his backyard grew so tall they blocked his view of Mount Rainier. Shadows fell for him earlier each day. Out of sight down by the back fence, he still had his horseshoe pits where he and Mr. Nordheim, his eighty-five-year-old neighbor, competed. Clear up at the house, you could hear the ringing and Mr. Nordheim swear in Norwegian.

At the end of his life, I'm sure my father thought I could fall out of most any boat and get back in, though I felt he stood close by and watched. I still feel that way. It's a comfort and a measure. After Penny and I were married, he gave me a scrapbook he had tended season by basketball season—my basketball records, team pictures, basketball articles from the *Tacoma News Tribune* and the *Spokesman Review*, programs of the games he'd attended, stat sheets, a whole history of my basketball career. He'd collected it all by himself as simply and as thoughtfully as he shored up my mother's gardens. This was the first I knew of it.

My mother must have asked him finally what he was doing sitting out in the car after dark with the neighbors watching. "Listening to Jim's game on the radio," he told her. When Washington State played in Oregon or Idaho or simply at home in Pullman, three hundred miles away, my father would sit in his driveway and search the car's radio for the game. It was the 1960s. AM radio was the band of choice, and when the ionosphere lifted after dusk, signals skipped in from a long way off. He'd drive until he found the game and the best reception and then park, invariably in front of his own house on that hill in Tacoma. Through the static and distance, he found me and listened by himself.

When I think of my father, I try to listen carefully. Throughout my growing up, "think, think," he would say, my tenpenny nails bent, a fender dented, another hasty choice based on too few facts. I'd listen hard to my thoughts fading in and out. "Slow down," he would say. This from a man, like many, who had worked his way through poverty and war. What I know is that he was deliberate and thoughtful and always there for me in his solitude—and then he wasn't. As often as I can, I string a rod and stand in a river. Or rent a boat to drift across a calm lake and fish until dusk. Or sometimes I simply drive late at night and listen to the radio. The reception is far better, then, for distant places and time.

FATHERS & FATHERING

JOHN ELDER

Pillow and Cradle

[*Note*: This selection comes from Elder's *Reading the Mountains of Home*, a book that relates Robert Frost's poem "Directive" to the human and natural history of the Green Mountains and integrates a memoir of one year in the life of the author's family. The following skein of passages relating to Elder's father and son begins in the book's fifth chapter and is completed in the twelfth, and final, one.]

The woods around this January beaver pond are a laboratory of succession—the pattern of continuity within change which was so central to Robert Frost's perception of nature. Next to the pond, where logging seems to have occurred most recently, stands a dense grove of red maples. These large, attractive hardwoods often precede sugar maples in the reforesting of moist, disturbed ground. They are quite similar to those more familiar cousins, except for the V's between sections of their leaves as opposed to the U's dividing the foliage of sugar maples. Yellow birches, smelling of wintergreen where little curls of bark peel off their trunks, are also mixed into these woods, as are a few ancient, slow-growing hemlocks.

On the other side of the pond, although there are few signs of logging, the ground is broken into a pronounced alternation of humps and hollows. Foresters call such a pattern of disturbed ground "pit and mound" or "pillow and cradle." It registers blow-down. When trees have toppled over, a half-circle of their roots tilts up into the air, exposing a hollow in the ground that remains even after the fallen log has begun to rot and the exposed roots have subsided into a softly contoured mound covered with soil and leaves. Our county forester, David Brynn, counsels me always to think of trees from the root-collar down. Remember, David says, that at least as much of a tree's biomass will generally be below the ground as is above it, with the root-circle of an old hemlock often spreading out for forty or fifty feet. Remember that even for the white pines which sink such a mighty taproot, an equal amount of root by weight is in the tiny filaments that spread their interwoven mat just below the topsoil's nutrient sink. Blow-down raises the hidden life of trees into the light.

I appreciate "pillow and cradle" as a phrase to describe this juxtaposition of a depression in the woods and a nearby hump of raised ground. It expresses the perpetual renewal within the rise and fall of individual trees. Another eloquent term is "nurse log," describing the way in which a fallen tree nourishes seedlings along its length, making its stored energies available to the ongoing life of the forest. Tom Wessels, who teaches field ecology at the Antioch Environmental Studies Program in New Hampshire, informs me that a fallen evergreen may decay, and nurse new life, over a period of sixty to seventy years, while a hardwood log may decompose and make itself available within a cycle of thirty to fifty years. In his essay "Ancient Forests of the Far West," from *The Practice of the Wild*, Gary Snyder celebrates the nourishing persistence of fallen elders: "And then there are some long subtle hummocks that are the last trace of an old gone log. The straight line of mushrooms sprouting along a smooth ground surface is the final sign, the last ghost, of a tree that 'died' centuries ago."

A fallen log is something for hope. Not a hope for personal immortality, and not an assurance of prosperity or any other form of individual security. A hope, rather, for involvement in the grand pattern that connects. The southward orientation of many pillow-and-cradle formations in the rising ground just west of here tells of another event that occurred in 1938, along with the death of Elinor Frost and Robert's move into the little cabin at the woods' edge. A hurricane swept through this part of New England, absolutely leveling thousands of acres. Pillows and cradles in identical alignment show me its tracks amid the trees of Bristol Cliffs. Seedlings quickly establish themselves in the full light and nutrient-rich litter of such a vast blow-down. In disaster, they have discovered grounds for hope.

I visited my father in Hillhaven Convalescent Home shortly before he died. His gaunt head was propped up on a lofty white pillow, and his arms looked thin and frail lying on top of the sheets. Looking at his arms, though, I thought of a day when I was a boy of six and he and I rowed a borrowed skiff way out into the Gulf of Mexico. The boat had been in storage for years, so that the bottom was dried out and leaky. Water began to well up, then suddenly rushed through the separating planks. Our boat sank with us too far from shore to even make out the white porch railings of our little vacation house. But my father calmly said to put my arms around his neck so that he could swim us in. I remember the total security I felt, resting on the smooth, powerful muscles of his back, watching the sweep of his arms through the brown water. I drowsed along, safe with my father above the invisible currents of the deep. I remembered that strength in Hillhaven, looking down at his thin arms and bony, age-spotted hands. I remember it now, in the life-and-death of this Vermont wilderness.

Death and life are both embodied in a nurse log. Nature is always unified for one who can let go and identify with a life that transcends individuality. But certain propositions are much easier to affirm in the abstract, and such letting go sometimes requires first being overturned and uprooted. Frost's first volume of poetry, *A Boy's Will*, was published in 1913. One stanza of "In Hardwood Groves" from that volume connects the need to fall back into the fund of life not only with blow-down but also with the annual descent of leaves.

> Before the leaves can mount again
> To fill the trees with another shade,
> They must go down past things coming up,
> They must go down into the dark decayed.

I feel Frost's struggle in the reiterated "must," as in the phrase "dark decayed." Decomposition at the bacterial level may be easier to contemplate if one leaves one's own body out of the picture. But only with an inclusive perspective on the universal breakdown of organisms can one look past it to new life. Only by adopting a time line that comprehends the visitations of glaciers and the rise and fall of whole forests may one draw the lesson home. This is the tough but liberating view of life taught by the memory-tangled, ever-new New England woods.

Without Frost, it would have been much harder for me to appreciate the human meaning of these woods. Growing up in northern California, I was within a bike ride of Muir Woods. That grove of redwoods was my criterion for natural integrity as I began to enjoy nature on my own. When I eventually moved east to attend graduate school, the woods of Connecticut left me feeling disappointed and disoriented. They seemed to lack the sublime beauty of the redwoods with their grand columns rising through the filtered light, their forest floor almost devoid of underbrush. Walking in a little patch of forest near Guilford, Connecticut, I felt how small the trees were, how little they conformed to the monolithic simplicity of the redwoods, and how littered the forest floor felt with its broken branches and leaf duff everywhere. I felt closed into a messy room rather than released into natural grandeur. Another grad student from the West repeated to me the libel, based on the relative smallness and proximity of landforms in this part of the country, that being in New England was like living in a teacup. Right, I thought, and in the tattered leaves that slid around my boots I'd found the dregs.

But Frost offers a vision of sublimity based not on spaciousness and noble clarity but rather on endurance in the face of loss, unity in fragmentation, and the warmth of decay. These are primarily physical truths for him, not metaphysical ones. Snow covers and temporarily arrests the decomposition of this forest floor, but beneath it lie the vestiges of several successive growing seasons. The top layer—"fit[ting] the earth like a leather glove," as Frost has it at the beginning of "In Hardwood Groves"—is composed of the brown but intact leaves of the previous fall. Beneath them is a layer of fragments and skeletons, sometimes just the spines of leaves, or the tips, or the outlines of maple or red oak leaves defining a webwork of holes. Just below those shards, and yet another year earlier, are found the crumbly little indistinguishable scraps, the chaff of three seasons' winnowing. And then comes the sweet black dirt. This soil is the "dark decayed," a layer of renewal from which sweet nutrients seep down into the mineral mix, food for the trees that overhang in familial continuity.

A forester named George Kessler introduced me to the concept of soil horizons. The decaying leaves and fragments mark the O, or organic, horizon, while the topsoil, lying beneath that fertile litter, is the A horizon. Below that comes the B horizon, or subsoil, which contains relatively little organic material. Slicing down into the forest floor, he showed me the lines of demarcation from the light brown of duff to the black of topsoil to the mineral-rich red-brown of the subsoil. New England, like the West, has its own big sky, but its horizons stretch beneath our boots. The circulation of water is like wind for this saturated soil. It bears leaves and ashes down through three horizons, then lifts them into trees that, even in early January, have their buds fully formed and ready to receive the spring.

Here I am back in Bristol, working in our barn as the afternoon of this long day draws to a close. A couple of shoplights shine down, plugged into an outlet on the deck with a long orange extension cord. A kerosene heater roars at my back and almost keeps me from shivering. I am drawing beads of glue along the edge of slender cedar strips, bending them around station-molds that establish the tapering contours of a canoe, and stapling them onto these molds in order to clamp them together, edge to edge, while the glue dries. All year, as I have been pursuing my hikes, I have also been stealing hours to work on this wooden canoe, as a project honoring my father's memory. It's a task considerably beyond my experience or skills, and one I would have never taken on had it not been for a dream.

Last August Rita and I were taking a two-day vacation on the coast, having dropped Caleb off at his youth-orchestra camp in New Hampshire and on our way to pick up Matthew from a canoeing camp in Maine. It was a rare time to relax together, and we spent most of one day strolling along the harbor in Camden and poking around in shops. One bookstore had a large section on sailing and boat construction, and I became fascinated by the books on canoe building. The next night we were in Portland and decided to go out to dinner for our twenty-fourth anniversary. This was stretching it, since it was only August 19th and the actual date was the 30th. But we weren't likely to have another evening so spacious as the beginning of school approached, and we had heard about an elegant little restaurant in the old part of town, called Alberta's Seafood Grill. The meal was in fact wonderful, the atmosphere warm and inviting. But throughout a very happy evening tears kept rolling down my cheeks, to my total surprise. It seemed funny, really, just an overflow of love.

That night, when we returned to our motel on the outskirts of town, I had a dream as vivid as the image of a clintonia blossom beside a trail. In it, a sleek cedar-strip canoe was floating on the water. Its mellow reddish-golden color especially struck me, along with its name, the *Tribute*, written in calligraphic script along the right side of the bow. I walked closer to the shore by which it hung and looked down at the smaller letters of the inscription on the bow-deck. It read "JLE" and below that, "1918–94." Around these letters and numerals were wreathed the words "of the current to the source," with "source" coming right around to the circle's beginning and making one continuous phrase. I wrote this dream down in my journal and told Rita about it, realizing that it was a kind of memorial to my father, still alive in Hillhaven Convalescent but in sad decline because of the progression of his Alzheimer's. This new link between him and one of my favorite lines from

"West-Running Brook" stirred me, since Dad had been much on my mind. The dream felt like an appropriate form of homage, but then it faded from my mind, like other nighttime revelations.

Two days later, having picked up Matthew, we pulled into our driveway in Bristol to find a message from my mother waiting for us. Dad had died on the evening of August 19th. Frost's poem of haunting gave me permission to believe Dad's spirit traveled to me that night in tears and a dream. But it also made me buy the book that told how such canoes were made, rig up a shop in our drafty barn, and begin to transform a long crate of wooden strips into the curved and symmetrical integrity of a hull. These thin, pliable planks, which I purchased from a marine supply company in Buffalo, have bead-and-cove edges—one convex and the other concave to hold the glue even when the strips wrap around a curve rather than joining in a plane. They make me think this evening of the pillow-and-cradle patterns of a forest floor—the juxtaposition of hummock and hole that tells the story of succession and that includes passing generations of trees in the present of a single slope.

At the farther end of North Mountain lies Bristol Pond, my favorite spot for canoeing. Building this craft, I have both remembered my father and imagined paddling the completed *Tribute* across the pond on a placid summer day. That would bring some closure to this year of grieving, as well as to the reading, hiking, and writing that have flowed together in this book. It would be a chance to reflect in quietness, after the effort and disorientation of the trail. But now I must bend back over the canoe's skeleton and partial hull, stretching my arms out as far as they'll go to hold a new strip of the curve firmly in place while I set a couple of staples near the craft's stern. As my stapler clacks, a sudden gust rattles the big barn doors. The kerosene heater gives a roar, bathes the canoe for a moment in its vivid glow, then dies back down.

Rita and I have been working through a fractured year in the life of our family. Our difficulty communicating with Matthew has been a particular source of worry. So when, early in July, Matthew told me that he wanted us to take the *Tribute* through Otter Creek Gorge together, there was nothing on earth that would have made me say no.

There was also just about no one else to whom I would have said yes. The *Tribute* was the gleaming product of a whole winter of work beside the hissing kerosene heater in the barn. It meant a great deal to me—as a memorial to my father, as by far the most ambitious wood-working project I'd ever completed, and as a promise of reflective soli-tude on Bristol Pond. Besides, Addison County had recently been swamped with heavy rains. I knew that below the steep rocks walls of Otter Creek Gorge the water would be exploding along over invisible rocks. My whitewater experience is minimal, and furthermore, I've never been particularly inclined to gain any more.

Matthew, on the other hand, did know something about running the rapids. A summer ago, as he began to move into his darker phase, we had sent him to a camp in Maine that specialized in wilderness ca-noeing. The last thing he said as we dropped him off for the month was, "I bet you hope this is going to change my attitude, don't you?" We did, and it didn't. But he learned a lot about paddling all the same, saw some wildlife, and got in great shape. This proposal was therefore a chance to acknowledge and enter Matthew's own area of expertise, even if I wasn't sure it was matched to the particular realities of our place and season. I hoped that when I said, "Sure, let's go!" he would be surprised by my failure to raise cautions or propose alternatives— my usual role from his perspective. It felt great to turn the governor off and, on this sunny Saturday, resolutely to ignore the little voice that was muttering, "This may not be such a smart idea."

I'd canoed through Otter Creek Gorge once before, in our old wide-bottomed fiberglass canoe. Even though the river was much lower for that fall outing, it was still a memorable rush, less like the skilled con-trol implied by "running the rapids" than like a roller-coaster ride which, once seated in my craft, I had no power to direct and hoped only to endure. Now, years later, I couldn't even remember exactly where we put in for this piece of the river. We finally decided to launch from the parking lot of a longtime Addison County institution called the Dog Team Tavern. While taking the canoe off our van, we noticed that guests were collecting outside the dining room for a wedding re-ception. Grandparently couples were chatting on the lawn that sloped down to the Otter, while boys in white shirts and bow ties and girls in flowered dresses played on the swings and high-glider. Matthew and I skulked down the lawn with the *Tribute* in our grubbies and caps, while the matrimonial party looked on with benign curiosity.

We were in a hurry to get our craft on the water, and were feeling conspicuous under all those eyes. But it was a hard place to start, with large boulders crowding our side of a strong curve in the river. We fi-nally clambered among them to a gravelly channel on the inner bend, slid into our tippy vessel, and pointed the bow downstream. This was the first sunny morning in several days, and the overhanging maples, cedars, and red pines were washed and glistening. We'd picked up a couple of sandwiches and iced teas at the Mobil in Bristol before starting. Matthew had eaten most of his lunch in the car, but I now pulled over to a shelf of rock out of sight of the Dog Team to eat my own, along with the economy-sized bag of barbecue potato chips that I was indulging in from the same spirit of license that let me in for this outing in the first place. Kingfishers were chattering over the water and bank swallows were arcing around them. As we sat on a sloping outcrop of granite we heard a train whistle, and looked up to watch the train snake over a trestle far above our heads. I'd forgotten that Matthew didn't particularly care for barbecue chips when making my purchase and, by this time, had eaten most of the bag myself. Between feeling glutted on chips and knowing that the actual gorge and rapids came right after the train's bridge, I was becoming decidedly uneasy.

We packed ourselves back in the canoe and shoved off into the current again, under the stolid eyes of several fishermen on nearby boulders, their lines pulled taut by the force of the muddy green water. The river was narrower now and the pull of its current mightier with each stroke of our paddles. As we approached a new bend we began to hear a low, pounding roar. I knelt in the bottom of our slim, low-riding craft, trying to establish as much stability as I could before we turned the corner. Reviewing the highly detailed chapter on whitewater strategy that I'd read last night in my *Complete Wilderness Paddler*, I realized suddenly this was all going to happen so fast that my strategy would be limited to keeping the bow pointing forward and hoping we didn't hit a big rock.

Given Matthew's greater experience with whitewater, we had decided he should be in the stern. This gave me an excellent view of the first portion of the gorge, in which our canoe was still actually above the water. The rapids seemed much higher and faster, and potentially more fatal, than those I'd seen in televised whitewater canoe and kayak competitions. It had apparently been possible for those competitors to read the locations of boulders from the mounds of water that foamed above them. But here it simply felt like an undifferentiated explosion of white, as if Moby Dick himself were bursting to the surface. There was absolutely no way I could figure out how to read the channel or steer a course. In fact I couldn't see more that a few feet ahead, couldn't make out either bank, and could just barely hear Matthew bellowing "Draw hard on the right!"

I could, however, feel the tremendous wallops as my gleaming memorial encountered some concrete details of this one real river on one particular day. And I could see, with the clarity of a dream, water washing straight over our high, arched prow. First, it pulsed over the bow deck whenever we hit an especially mighty standing wave, bathing the inscription to my father so that it glowed in the mellow light suffusing our misty world within the gorge. Then, as the bow began to take on more weight and dipped, the current began to flow steadily in around my knees, as at the turning of a tide. Our canoe never did tilt, turn, or capsize as in the illustrations of the paddling guide. Instead, after the river had lowered us a bit more, it simply shoved us straight under with its foamy hand.

Watching us sink from my end of that parade was a serene, quiet, and, on the whole, interesting experience—like watching a freeway guardrail glide slowly toward me when I once sat in a hopelessly skidding vehicle. But as soon as we were in the drink, the world of speed and noise switched on again. The canoe, Matthew, and I were all bounced down through the rocks at an incredible rate. I remember thinking that it was a good idea to keep our heads up, so that we'd simply wash over the tops of those gray lurkers. I remember regarding our half-submerged canoe with a friendly and companionable feeling. It felt more like a comrade now, propelled along beside us, its cedar planking lovely in the swirl. I remember Matthew shouting and laughing, the first laughter I had heard from him in months, and I remember yelling back. Something pointless and silly like "Hold onto your paddle!" or "I'll meet you at the eddies." It felt great to be in the grip of that rushing water and, dangerous as the moment might have been, there wasn't a worry in my mind.

The river did begin to broaden and slow, but even after we found our footing and began to drag the *Tribute* toward shore, it was difficult to climb out. The upstream eddies were in fact really powerful, so much so that it was a challenge just to keep standing in the waist-deep water, much less to pull ourselves and the canoe out. When we finally managed to raise the *Tribute* high enough to empty all the water, the going became easier. We could hold on to the rails on either side, push off with our feet, and glide into the bank at an angle accommodating the eddies' force.

These remarkable eddies reflected not only the sudden broadening of Otter Creek after its frenzied tumult in the gorge but also the fact that we had just reached the confluence of the creek and the New Haven River. The New Haven pours its waters into the Otter placidly, and with a calming effect, here at River's Bend. After that, the combined streams proceed through Vergennes to connect up with the northward flow of Dead Creek before debouching into Lake Champlain. I sat on the muddy promontory where the Y of separation joined at the stem of convergence and watched Matthew steering the *Tribute* up and down the Otter's rapids. He skillfully read the eddies' backward pull and rode upstream with minimum paddling. Then, shielded from the main roar of waters by a rocky point, he carefully aligned the *Tribute* before thrusting out into the melee and flinging back downstream toward my paternal somnolence. He was wearing my red Gore-Tex hat with the broad black brim. It shone in the brightening afternoon sun. . . . Matthew moved briskly, purposefully, and happily in the middle distance, as I lounged on the shore, heart calmly slowing, and never taking my eyes off him.

When I first set out to walk the ridges above Bristol and make myself at home, I never anticipated the convulsions this year would bring to our family. The losses of Frost's farm family and the disappearances of whole communities among these mountains had engaged me on a more intellectual level. But the photographs on my study bookshelf map a story of grief that has colored my narrative of hiking and reading the heights. In the small portrait of my parents, they are dressed up as if for church, my mother with her signature pearl earrings and necklace, and wearing a navy blue dress. My father wears a dark suit, white shirt, and maroon tie. They are both smiling serenely into the camera. When this photo was taken, they were already retired but had not yet begun to experience any physical decline. Now my mother is recovering very slowly from an operation and my father is dead. Grieving doesn't seem to have an end. Yet there they are in the picture, wise and content, patiently waiting for me to comprehend the watershed within which they still circulate through my life.

An even older picture leans beside that one on the bookshelf. It was taken during a sabbatical in Berkeley fifteen years ago, and shows Rita and the children on the deck behind our rented house. Rita's hair was

jet-black and, although I can see the wedding ring on her finger, she looks just as I remember her from her junior year in college. Rachel's a four-year-old, with those pink-rimmed, coke-bottle-thick glasses that she used to wear. With both hands, she proudly holds out on display the little flowered skirt Rita had sewn for her. Rita's down on one knee holding up Caleb, who's wearing little sneakers with his overalls but is not yet at the point of standing by himself. Sitting in the center with his yellow turtleneck and with rainbow suspenders for his jeans, and looking remarkably like the trademark Dutch Boy of the paint company, is Matthew. Whereas my parents' picture was taken when they were about fifteen years older than Rita and I are now, this family portrait from Berkeley was taken just about that long *ago*. So the center of the whole familial array is now. In the midst of all this grief and confusion, "Here are your waters and your watering place."

Which swirls me back once more to "Directive," Frost's topographical map of home. Reading it has been a way both to hike these mountains around our family's home and to tell the story of our own generations. The poet has shown me that wholeness beyond confusion comes through, and within, getting lost enough to find yourself. He has offered a series of maps, each of which has a spot in it for this moment in the life of our family. He has told a long story of geology and settlement within which our familial narrative is placed and magnified. He cautions me to resist the simplifying impulse of "Back out of all this now," and instead to flow back continually into the losses and the waters of this place.

Crickets chirr tentatively outside the study window, tuning up for the throbbing, late-August choruses that consummate the summer and conclude the singers' lives. Asters and goldenrod bloom along the unmowed roadsides of our town, while jewelweed and nettles intertwine in the weedy patch behind our barn. In another couple of months, we'll hear a distant calling and rush out into our driveway to watch flotillas of snow geese and Canada geese soaring southward with the turning year. They'll go right above that hogback ridge, reversing my whole northward trek within just a few minutes of their flight. My hike through "Directive" has helped me identify with the losses and recoveries, the migrations and returns, that are the living circulation of our family's place on earth.

BERND HEINRICH

Contact

Think of our life in nature,—daily to be shown matter, to come in contact
with it,—rocks, trees, wind on our cheeks! the *solid* earth! the *actual*
world! the *common sense! Contact! Contact! Who* are we? *where* are we?

HENRY DAVID THOREAU

Fathering is for me right now an active concern, and the natural world
is central to it because that world is my children's heritage. My wife,
Rachel Smolker, and I have two kids, Lena age two, and Eliot age four,
and we wish them the early exposure that we were fortunate to have.
Like me, Rachel grew up with a coterie of wild pets of the kind that still
fill our moments with joy and beauty. None were ever caged. All were
free to roam with us—crows, hawks, a jay, a flicker, coons, squirrels, a
skunk. We encourage the nature interests the children already express.
There is hardly a day when I come home after work that Eliot does not
run up to me beaming broadly and saying "Look Daddy" . . . "I found
a red eft," or a toad, another frog, another kind of snake, or a water beetle, or cranefly. We never tell him to go out and catch things, but we
genuinely share his enthusiasm whenever he does.

He has been comfortable holding and handling all sorts of animals
since at least two years of age. It started with earthworms. At age one
or earlier he spent hours finding and handling them in the garden. At
age three he wanted to keep everything he found. Now, with our urging, empathy is dawning, and except for a few special finds he releases
the snakes, newts, turtles, frogs, and toads after a day or two. His current passion is insects. To encourage him with genuine enthusiasm I've
started my own insect collection. It reconnects me to my own childhood, and my relearning allows me to tell him the names of things that
he asks, constantly. He contributes to my collection, and I to his; so we
swap specimens. It is, of course, necessary that I show him the basics:
how to kill insects in the freezer and how to pin them. He has his own
net and collection case. Our kitchen table is now covered with jars and
aquaria, as he tries to rear every caterpillar he finds to the adult moth

or butterfly. He often fails, and so do I. Mistakes are not a problem. No learning is possible without making mistakes. Sometimes a jar with foliage is taken out and left in the sun, and it overheats. A cover may be left off and the leaves are not moist enough or not changed often enough. A caterpillar is handled too much. There is not the proper soil for pupation of a noctuid moth, no twigs provided for an emerging nymphalid butterfly to hang when it needs to spread its limp wings, or no leaves are left for a saturnid moth to spin its cocoon into.

We made a survey of what he caught, handled, and ultimately identified and learned something about during one day at camp last weekend. The partial list includes three green snakes, two red-bellied snakes, two garter snakes, one toad, wood frogs and green frog tadpoles, a crayfish, one water beetle, water striders, several caterpillars, flies, beetles, butterflies, spiders, and ants. Every day he must catch some bugs to feed other bugs or his snake. He sees me raise moths from eggs, through larvae, to pupae, to adults that after laying hundreds of eggs are eaten by a bird. It pays off. I can say with confidence that he already knows more about the local fauna, and maybe the natural world, than 98 percent of the biology majors in my Biology 2 lecture hall at the local university. On the one hand that scares me. On the other it gives hope, because so little can do so much.

My first child, a daughter, grew up in California suburbia. We had the usual pets—a cat, a dog, and at times also birds. She developed an appreciation for living things and became an honors student in biology, and went on to complete medical school. For a graduation present, we explored and camped in Costa Rica. My nephew Charlie is a surrogate son who has been my deer-hunting companion since he was a high school student. He graduated from Bowdoin College in Maine, and after his Ph.D. from the University of North Carolina, we went on a month-long canoe trip down the Noatac River in Alaska. We fished for arctic char and grayling, watched birds and wolves, and camped on the sand banks in the tundra. We spend the last week of November every year full-time in the Maine woods. His expertise is environmental toxicology, and he loves the woods, streams, and knows what's in them. He knows when specific mayflies hatch and where, and how many grouse a woods is likely to hold. His brother Chris, an organic chemist, is also an outdoor enthusiast.

My second child, a son, is about to graduate from high school. Stuart is also an honors student. He grew up with his mother, a computer scientist, and perhaps as a result has grown up with less intimate nature contact. He is, it seems to me, swallowed up in the world of computers, where he finds his information, social interactions, and his entertainment. He has a huge and precious gift for artistic expression, but instead he has spent endless hours at computer games that (as far as I can tell) serve up screen violence that is supposed to be entertainment. Can this be a healthy diet for a developing mind? We are what we eat. But he knows more about computers than I ever will.

Like all my children, Stuart started to be interested in dinosaurs and insects while he was still with me in the toddler stage, but like my sisters and older daughter his connections to the natural world are now more like those of the norm in our culture. He has no interest in finding out what kinds of critters might lurk in the local bog, where the fisher's tracks might lead in the snow; nor does he care to hunt or fish. I do not mind that he doesn't, although I of course feel he is missing out on much that the natural world has to offer. Perhaps I have failed him in not helping him forge that bonding to the outdoors, to specific place and all that is in it.

Like ravens and many other intelligent animals, we grow up keying in very early to whatever is of interest or practically relevant to those around us. In the past, next to our fellows, the living environment has always been the most important aspect of our immediate lives. It is unlikely that young Homo sapiens is content to "leave only footprints" or perchance "stay in the paths and take only pictures" as an uninvolved observer, as we are often instructed. That's not how humans have been enticed by evolution to experience the world, because that's not how for over 4 million years we have evolved. We're utilitarian creatures.

In our ever-more urbanizing culture, the connections with nature are dissolving and our common understanding of nature is dropping precipitously, even as appreciation of life is increasing. However, life is now commonly experienced atomized and out of context, as though it begins at point A and ends at point X. You get the kind of mentality of those who say idiotic things like "life begins at conception." I've actually *heard* that on the public radio. (Of course life began 4 billion years ago, and it has no beginning and it has no end. It is a process, in which matter gets interconverted endlessly, being recycled. You never get something from nothing. Not even knowledge, or love, or wisdom, or orioles, or king snakes, or immunity, or toughness.) We see individual *lives* rather than an ecologically interdependent process that can be experienced only when the world is seen simultaneously through the senses and deduced from the reactions of thousands of different animals. In contrast, when viewing everything from a human or even a dog's or a deer's perspective, our outlook becomes myopic although all the more personal and strong, and ignorance then commonly masquerades as morality.

Our connections to nature and our understanding of it are forged by working contact, as opposed to voyeurism. Otherwise, nature becomes compartmentalized, and ultimately peripheral and uninteresting. A thousand slick films of beautiful carabid beetles and all the textbooks in the world cannot substitute for finding even one real beetle in the forest so unexpectedly under a pile of moss in a pit trap dug by one's father—capturing it, smelling it, watching it, identifying it, and perhaps ultimately also having it to keep. All necessary steps in order to anchor the beetle into the emotionally based memory processes. As Rachel Carson put it: "Exploring nature with your child is largely a matter of becoming receptive to what lies around you." But why should any child become receptive? To try to answer that, I go back to my own childhood.

I remember retrieving live mice, shrews, and carabid beetles from under the cushions of moss that my father placed into the bottoms of pit traps he had dug into the soil in our woods. He had taken me along on his daily rounds to check these traps. He told me that by providing the moss the mice would spend less time trying to dig or jump out. He was so careful not to leave any dangling roots. We put the mice into little white cloth bags to collect the fleas that were sold to the Rothschilds in London. My mother made museum skins to be sold to the American Museum, and we ate the meat. Papa showed me how to pin and correctly name, label, and store the beetles for my collection in which the carabids were far and away my favorites. The beetles entranced me.

I got more instructions on the habits of small forest mammals when we went trapping with snap traps. Papa was meticulous in setting every single trap at just the right spot where it might catch a certain kind of mouse or shrew. Those spots became magical. I still remember the specific bend of the brook where under the bank he caught a mouse that he did not expect to find there.

I was between four and ten years old at the time, and my mind is still filled with vivid pictures where I see less of my father than the nature that he led me to see. One picture is of a mossy bank along a brook, 75 under beech trees, where he and I were pulling up moss. I found an especially exciting ichneumon wasp, subfamily Ichneumoninae, in hibernation. This one was gun-barrel blue with white spots, and he had only one in his collection. He wanted it. He needed it. That made it important and therefore remembered and distinguished from Cryptinae, Pimplinae, and all the rest. In *The Sense of Wonder*, Rachel Carson expressed what I felt: "I am sure no amount of drill would have implanted the names so firmly as just going through the woods in discovery."

Papa did not go out into the woods except for a purpose. Or perhaps more truthfully, he likely rationalized a purpose because he wanted to be out in them whenever he could. He took me along, never my one-year-younger sister, perhaps because I was more active and interested (although it is difficult to sort out cause and effect). There was then too much serious business of eking out a living to think of partitioning what we were doing daily into play or education versus living. To me the living was play.

We lived then, right after the war, for nearly six years in a one-room cabin hidden deep in a forest in northern Germany. Of course we had no electricity or conveniences such as radios, TV, newspapers, or books. Consequently, I never saw animals depicted as humanoid cartoon characters as is commonly done now for entertainment. Instead, my sisters and I were enchanted listening to my father's adventure stories as we lay next to him in the evening before going to sleep. I'm certain he never made up anything fanciful. His stories were gripping because they were, to the smallest detail, as real as any carabid beetle in my collection. I was especially entranced by his adventures in Bulgarian swamps, where the birds were rare and secretive, and the rails were incredibly hard to see.

I was ten years old when we left there and came to live in rural Maine. It was a big transition that changed much, even and perhaps especially the relationship with my father. Almost everything that happened thereafter tended to pull us apart: my life became increasingly a different world. Indeed, after a year my parents left for six years to go on expeditions, first to Mexico and then to Angola in Africa. We were dropped off at a school for disadvantaged, mostly homeless kids. Reaching puberty, I wanted to associate with and be accepted by other kids. My father, when he was around before that, and later after I'd gone to college, wanted me to go with him to collect his beloved ichneumon wasps. But I started to see him as I imagined others saw him—

a foreigner who was slightly odd because he wore white shorts and carried a butterfly net. I became more interested in the nature pursuits of our neighbors and adopted one and possibly two of these neighbors as new father figures, and they adopted me.

My surrogate fathers were outdoorsmen (when they were not working in the local woolen mill or on their farms), which in rural Maine meant they chased coons and rabbits with hounds, lined bees, fished for trout, and hunted deer. Catching a ten-inch brookie, finding the biggest bee tree, or getting a ten-point buck might have been the lure that made the woods important and exciting, but ultimately what stuck with me longest was the sense of adventure and the taste and feel of the woods. Hunting and fishing brought companionship with adults, but they also offered me a sense of contentment while I was alone in the woods often from dawn till dark. Constant intense listening and looking, with all senses alert to the smallest nuances, deepened my long immersion in maple ridges and swamps. It brought ever greater familiarity and affinity with birds, insects, mice, and moose. I believe all of us who have access to the outdoors, often as a relief from boredom or hard work, develop an addiction to it, because nature, although it seeps in slowly, eventually resonates with the heart. I longed to live in the woods forever, imagining an idyllic existence living in a cabin along a stream and close to animals.

Shortly after my parents dropped me off at boarding school (permanently, it seemed) so they could travel to other continents, I gave away the little microscope my father had given me as a present. I stopped collecting insects and played baseball and other sports instead. Nevertheless, my nature interests were hard to kill. They were just redirected. I loved to be out in the woods, and escaped there as much as I possibly could from my tormenting, regimenting, and religionizing housemother. My six years at this school were very hard, and I hate to think what could have happened to me if it were not for the school's beautiful surrounding wild lands of forests, streams, and river (the Kennebec).

My father had wanted me to take over his ichneumonid collection, in the name of tradition, and was disappointed that I showed no interest, or aptitude. I made a break from tradition as he perceived it to be and still feel sorry that I disappointed him. However, despite my lingering sadness and regret that as we grew older we grew apart, I'm ever mindful that at the most critical time of my life, he and others fostered an early exposure to the natural world that has nourished me ever since.

Through their enthusiasm my mentors transferred to me, unwittingly I suspect, the thrill they felt in contact and interaction, whether capturing a fabulous wasp, finding and felling a bee tree to expose the honey and the wonders of the hive, or stalking a deer. They, in effect, turned what could have been of neutral emotional content into fabulous experiences with amazing creatures, releasing a flood of endorphins in my brain. They showed me how to be at home in the woods and to become attuned to the nuances of the habits and needs of its inhabitants. They exposed me to the environment that we've evolved in, that we've perhaps been predisposed to be imprinted on. Fathers have done so since before we were even human when they took their growing children with them into the great world of their hunt.

My father did not treat either of his daughters as he did his son, and neither daughter developed along the trajectory that I did. One who was close to my grandmother, a painter of flowers, became a secretary to a baking firm in Chicago and liked to raise flowers. The other daughter became an elementary schoolteacher in Maine. Neither exhibited an intimate, almost intuitive feel for the wild natural world that is contingent on prolonged contact with it when still very young. Would my kids or possibly my students?

Several years ago I helped teach a course for high school teachers intended to show them how to pass on nature consciousness to their students. If I made any point on our mutual field trips beyond the need to observe closely, it was to contact intimately. I led them to grackle, sparrow, and starling nests. I encouraged them to *hold* the eggs, the young. *Look* at them. *Feel* them. *See* how the adults react. A friend who has done much to restore peregrine populations insists on doing the same when he brings kids and peregrines together, even though he knows it is technically illegal. Sadly, but perhaps predictably, in the evaluations afterward I was taken to task by two of these teachers for disturbing nature. They will continue to teach distancing to their students, not a fostering of contact. They think sentimentally, not ecologically. All courses that hope to teach awareness should incorporate some project—be it to survey the local beetle fauna, or determine the productivity of a stream—where the students get to do something important and practical, and maybe have fun getting muddied.

My older son, Stuart, the one obsessed with computers, was sent by his mother to Audubon camp. The well-meaning young nature instructor was impeccably pure and high-mindedly nature-loving. She tried to get the children to tiptoe through the woods, to instill in them such a deep reverence for life that they would shoo off the mosquitoes, who also need to eat, rather than kill them. Sure, it's a great thought, for an ideal world. But my son said he hated it. No wonder. Even before I was his age I was out in the swamp, shooting frogs with my slingshot or bow and arrows to feed my pet crow, Jacob. I was riding on the back of the neighbor's haymower to jump off and kill the field mice for my two tame sparrow hawks, or netting grasshoppers for my snakes. Since that Audubon experience my son has not shown any inclination to want to be out in the woods. It just wasn't fun. Now, almost a decade and a half later, we signed our four-year-old Eliot up for a week session at the same camp. Instead of being taken out to catch bugs immediately, the kids were gathered around in a circle and lectured. He didn't like the bird watching, because he could not contact the birds. He said they found only one daddy longlegs, and he got into an argument on whether daddy longlegs are spiders. He also asked me, "Why don't other people catch bugs?" After this, his first session there, he refused to go again, and insisted we take him to the brook to look for crayfish, bugs, and salamanders. Our critical programming for nature may occur at a very early age. *Now* was the time for him to make contact, even if it sometimes has proximate costs to the things we love.

Lena, our two-year-old, is currently hugging a baby chick nearly, if not totally, to death. She reminds me of how a day-care lady we know got her attitude about birds as a toddler. "I had a bad childhood experience," she says. "A bird flew into my hair. It was horrible. I don't mind watching a bird, but touching one gives me the willies." Who will vote for a swamp full of mosquitoes, or for bird habitat? It seems to me that if we want to *promote* constant development and environmental degradation, then there is one sure simple solution: make it illegal to harm or mess with any wild creatures, and tell the children they must "leave only footprints" and under no circumstances wander from the designated footpath. The don't-swat-it-catch-it-eat-it-touch-it school of thinking makes nature a frozen museum exhibit.

It boils down to the fact that nature is not a museum piece to keep one's grubby paws off. Nor is it a fuzzy chick to be hugged and cuddled. We have a need to be *in* nature. It's life to be lived and engaged in at every level. Unless actively discouraged, such contact comes to us naturally enough. Most youngsters start that engagement by catching bugs and worms and so on, and then, if they are not turned off by well-meaning adults who try to "educate" them, they graduate to having wild pets. They go through the catching-frogs-and-snakes phase, to rearing young birds, raccoons, skunks, and others. If this avenue is shut off or not encouraged, they may still become connected to the land, to nature, through hunting and fishing, as were most of the great conservationists of yesteryear. Now, due to lack of opportunity, social pressures, conservation laws designed principally for easing law enforcement to protect a few key species at the expense of people's contact with all the rest, and distracting alternative entertainment and lifestyles, most areas of active contact are being denied. Nature is becoming increasingly off-limits and thus a spectator sport, rather than an engagement with Life. I believe this trend, which nature writer Robert Michael Pyle calls the "extinction of experience," to be as dangerous as the extinction of species, because one leads to the other.

From my limited experience in Western society, it seems to me that in the past it was primarily boys who became more ecologically rooted to the natural world, because they and not their sisters were the ones who were taken out into the forests and fields and onto the streams and lakes. They were the ones who were responsible for attending to the needs of the farm animals, and who needed to learn the habits and intricacies of wild animals in order to bring meat to the table. They were the ones who got to experience nature, and to become attuned to its subtleties through venues other than pure sentimentality. They learned to get under the animal's skin, to access its life's requirements, feelings, and mentality. They learned that there is a thousand times more out there than can be seen in weeks of careful looking. To these ends, every child should be encouraged to find, and to have, a variety of wild pets. Only wild animals will connect them to the natural world; they are the child's best hope for direct and intimate contact. Will abuses result? Of course. (Just as in child rearing.) But learning nature is like learning to write—you've got to practice, and that means making mistakes. *No progress is possible without the total freedom to make mistakes.* Deny that (the cost) and you deny any and *all* chances for deep practical understanding. The cost of learning must, of course, be minimized—common sense is a requirement. Blanket rules are totally inadequate. The world is *not* black and white; *most* of it is hued in between. The only real evil is when any one thing, idea, position, is extrapolated ad infinitum, even in the direction that is just.

In the modern world, where the opportunities for contact are increasingly shrinking, and the necessity of maintaining contact is becoming increasingly important, the connections to the natural world may now no longer be automatic. Special effort will be required to provide that contact. That effort must start *long* before puberty, probably closer to infancy. And the key is pointed, specific education through parents, parental figures, and teachers the child respects and loves. We fathers cannot teach anything about the natural world except if the kids first see us as friends, and if we are actively and enthusiastically involved with and in nature perhaps even *for ourselves* first. Otherwise the child will immediately know it is unimportant. Walking in the woods *is* important, if we can find good rationalizations for it, so that we want to and want to badly. As Henry David Thoreau pointed out well over a century ago, doing so means bucking the trends of entrenched domesticated Homo sapiens: "If a man walks in the woods for love of them half of each day, he is in danger of being regarded as a loafer; but if he spends his whole day as a speculator, shearing off those woods and making Earth bald before her time, he is esteemed an industrious and enterprising citizen."

Ecologically, death is an important part of life. However, individual deaths resulting from too close contact with nature are not the problem. It's our large-scale ecological destruction that's the problem—the clear-cutting of forests for quick profit or farms, bulldozing farms to make more malls, buying useless trinkets that cause economic growth rather than creating stability. It was not those who walked the meadow to pick the flowers who put in the new development or yet another mall. It was those who didn't. It was not those who hunted ducks in the marsh who drained it. It was those who didn't. It is not those who hunt deer who want to clear-cut the woods. It is those who have spent little time in them. In my opinion, a father taking his son fishing for sunfish or newts, or hunting for deer or dragonflies, is not part of the problem. He is part of the solution. As Baba Dioum, a Senegalese conservationist stated: "In the end, we will conserve only what we love, we will love only what we understand, and we will understand only what we are taught."

I thank Timothy Otter for reading this essay and making many useful suggestions, and I'm grateful to Charlie, Chris, Stuart, Erica, Eliot, and Lena for their enduring enthusiasm.

MARK MENLOVE

The Sound of Water

I hold an image of my father, fifty feet up, his long, blue-jeaned legs hugging a narrow tree trunk as he loops a length of chain to which he will attach the thick rope for our swing. The image takes on a tactile sense of smooth wood under my bare feet: the landing for the swing, built up from the stream bank, is made of redwood decking so soft it dents under a fingernail yet resilient enough to withstand seasons of winter snow, spring floods, and summer heat. As near as memory allows me to pinpoint, my father is forty-three, maybe forty-four, in this mental snapshot.

I am a father now, approaching the age my father was when he made the rope swing. I wish for my son the sensation of squealing through a whoosh of cool air, legs scissored and hands clenched tight as he sails far out over the opposite bank. But circumstances are different. My son lives with his mother, hundreds of miles and another country away. I see him only in short visits of a few weeks at a time.

One of the things, I am sure, that drew my parents to the place we lived for most of my youth was the stream that bordered the property. Cottonwood trees towered above both banks. River birch and dogwood filled in the understory. The shimmering green wall of summer changed to a mosaic of brilliant yellows and dull reds in autumn and skeletal gray fingers in winter. Some of the birch and dogwood were there when we arrived, but much of it my father transplanted from a few miles upstream. He loved the look of those trees. Shiny red bark of river birch and delicate white flowers of dogwood complemented the liquid reflections of multicolored river rocks. I went with him, though I was too young to be of any help, when he dug saplings to transplant along our stretch of streambank.

In southern Arizona, where I live now, that stream would qualify as a river. But as one of many streams flowing out of Utah's Wasatch Mountains, it is known as Little Cottonwood Creek. I always thought it odd that our stream was named Little Cottonwood, when it flows higher and faster than Big Cottonwood Creek, which headwaters in the next canyon over. In Utah vernacular, we simply called it "the crick."

River gorges are not the only things shaped by running water. Little Cottonwood Creek was a constant in my life. Except during spring runoff, when it became a raging torrent, we kids could easily wade across it. At the tail end of the runoff, when the current was down but still swift and strong enough to pin a skinny body against a submerged log or low-lying branch, we floated the creek on inner tubes. My parents would often come along on these floats, one of them shuttling us in the back of a pickup truck to a drop-off point upstream and the other accompanying us as we floated back home. My mother would shriek and giggle and kick her feet in the icy water. My father would mostly just grin. Each summer we stacked smooth rocks to dam the water for a swimming hole. I would open my eyes underwater and will myself to swim close to the deep undercut banks with their shadowy black water and tangle of roots. I caught minnows by the bucketful and snatched dancing long-legged bugs we called water skeeters off the still surface. During winter we skated on the places where the ice was smooth.

The absence of flowing streams in the landscape I now inhabit is disconcerting. I never sleep more soundly than when I am within earshot of running water. That sound, soothing and ever present, is the backdrop of my youth. I wish I could provide a thing as constant as Little Cottonwood Creek for my son through his growing up years.

Like me as a boy, Logan loves to be outside. On his visits he spends hours digging in the gravel of our Tucson backyard, and he loves our walks in the surrounding desert. One might think this landscape would be disorienting compared to the high Canadian plains and mountains near Calgary where he lives, but he seems at ease here and likes to tell people he meets about the differences between Calgary and Arizona. He knows the names of prickly pear, saguaro, and cholla cacti. On a hike not long ago he was mesmerized when friends showed us a secret den they had discovered earlier, and the resident desert tortoise poked its head out.

At the edge of Little Cottonwood Creek, my father built us a tree house. I like to remember it as a project we all took part in, my two brothers and I working under his tutelage as he patiently taught us to measure out the entire structure first, then place each board precisely before nailing it, and finally to stagger the rows of cedar shake shingles on the roof, but I suspect the reality is my brothers and I were earnest onlookers at best. It isn't that we weren't allowed or encouraged to hammer and tinker—just the prior year my father had finished building the house we lived in, and there were plenty of wood scraps and castoff nails that we could flail away at with our very own hammers—but his sense of aesthetics required a certain decorum of the tree house. It would become a permanent fixture in his backyard, which bore the stamp of his balanced and orderly nature. My brothers and I were all younger than ten years old at the time. A ragtag jumble of misfit lumber such as we would have hammered together if left to our own devices simply would not do. I picture my brothers and not my sisters in this tree house memory, but that is a function of age, not gender. My two older sisters were teenagers at that time and more interested in boys and the society of peers than in backyard goings-on. Next in the sibling lineup was a succession of three brothers, of which I am the middle, followed by two more sisters who were not yet born when the tree house was constructed. My two younger sisters, running in the tracks of three brothers and immersed in that world of fast-flowing water and Tarzan swings, grew up capable and confident of their place in the outdoors.

Supported on each corner by a sturdy cottonwood trunk, the tree house perched over the creek in the path of the good cool air that followed the streambed down from the mountains. Between my brothers and me and our neighborhood companions, we kept the place occupied almost constantly. Summer nights would often find three or four of us stretched out in flannel-lined sleeping bags, our hushed voices swaying over the sounds of feathered leaves and marbled water.

Early on, the tree house served as our base for mock army fights and science-fiction adventures, late-night raids on the Petersens' raspberry patch, and other boyish mischief like soaping car windows or stringing toilet paper through neighbors' trees and yards. As we grew older the tree house shouldered increasingly fascinating and exotic endeavors. The summer between seventh and eighth grades, I learned to kiss there. Cindy Ingersol. Her spearmint-flavored tongue pushing into my mouth was unexpected, though not unpleasant. A few days after that encounter, a classmate who was between bouts of going steady with Cindy approached me and said he heard I had slept with her. I knew "slept with" was a euphemism for having sex, my notion of which was hazy at best, but I was pretty sure what Cindy and I had done—a few long unsloppy kisses and a couple of tentative though well-aimed hand passes over the outsides of T-shirts—didn't count. Even so, I smiled and said nothing.

I would gather the details of sex, mostly secondhand and not always accurate but close enough to get the general idea, over the next several years. By the time my father, at the prompting of my mother during a conversation that I overheard, got around to volunteering to explain the birds and the bees, I felt pretty well informed and I told him so. He was visibly relieved. The conversation turned to basketball.

Looking back, he must have known before he broached the topic that I had some notion of sexual basics since he had a short time before discovered a stack of porn magazines, including a how-to manual of grainy photographs, in a footlocker in my older brother Doug's room. Surely he knew I had poured over those pages too. The discovery of the stash is an infamous episode in our family lore. Jenny Hilton, who was best friends with my sister Sharla—they couldn't have been more than seven at the time—was saying her nightly prayers with her mother when she blurted out, "and please, Heavenly Father, don't make me look at any more of those nasty pictures at the Menloves' house." How Sharla and Jenny found the magazines I still don't know, but that prayer was answered with a chain of phone calls that culminated in a full-scale search of our bedrooms. Doug, who had been miserly with his glossy possessions, took the fall. He came home from school one day to find the entire assortment arranged on his bed. Paper-clipped to one of the covers was a note in my father's handwriting that said, "Let's talk." If there were fireworks in the ensuing conversation, I did not hear them. More likely, the tone was steady, the words barely punctuated.

Fortunately, at least in my hormone-charged eyes, my parents' search fell short on one count. Several old cushions, gleaned from someone's abandoned sofa, served as the only furniture in the tree house. In the center of each, accessed through a zipper on the side and then inserted into a carefully cut slice in the foam padding, lay two or three worn and wrinkled magazines. These were rejects from Doug's collection, either studied to the point they had lost their allure or simply not up to his standards. After the purge of the main house, Doug, who didn't frequent the tree house much by then, let it be known he was not taking the blame if these were discovered.

The cushion hiding place worked well for secreting packs of cigarettes too. We'd hoard them to smoke late at night, passing a single cigarette around a circle of three or four of us. One calm night, it would have been around 1 A.M., I had just tossed a butt into the stream below when the tree house shifted slightly under the weight of someone climbing the iron pegs that led to the trapdoor. Tobacco smoke hung on the heavy summer air as my father's head and shoulders appeared in the floor opening. A career air traffic controller, he was just getting home after working a late shift. From the driveway he must have smelled cigarettes and immediately known the source. He didn't climb all the way into the tree house. With only his upper body visible, he rested an elbow on the wood floor and leaned there for a moment. "Pretty late, isn't it?"

"Yeah," I replied. "We're just going to bed."

"Well, okay then. See you in the morning."

My father is a devout Mormon, a religion in which tobacco and alcohol are forbidden. I didn't need to be told that a thirteen-year-old smoking cigarettes rubbed against his grain.

There were other times. The year I turned sixteen, my older sister Peggy celebrated her college graduation by spending the summer in Guatemala with her Peace Corps boyfriend. She left her red '66 Mustang in my care. "I won't be too late," I called up the stairs as I was leaving the house one Friday evening. "Not too late" is a perfect phrase in the mind of a teenager. It is relative and easily defended after the fact. As I was getting into the car my father approached me.

"What can you tell me about the beer in the trunk?" he asked.

I blanched. An obvious lie would only make things worse. "Umm, it's mine."

"Where did it come from?"

"I bought it from a guy at school."

"How did he get it?"

"I don't know; I think from his brother."

I was unwilling to risk the obvious lie, but I was not above the more easily concealed variety. I had stolen the beer from Albertson's, where I worked as a grocery bagger. Vance, a wormy eighteen-year-old checkout clerk, taught me the ruse: One of my duties, to be done just before the end of a shift, was to stack empty milk crates outside the loading dock at the back of the store. Behind the crates, I'd hide two cases of beer, one for Vance and one for me. After work I'd drive behind the store and throw my case in the trunk. Not sophisticated enough to steal good beer, I'd take Coors Light or Hamms Draft.

Few things would cause my father greater disappointment than stealing or lying. I took the easy road, owning up to the contraband beer, but dodged responsibility for what I knew would be the greater sin in his eyes.

He sat on the hood of the car and cleaned his fingernails with the blade of his black-handled pocketknife. "I know there are things you're going to want to try for yourself," he said, "but you're awfully young to be drinking, and doing it while you're driving is just plain stupid." He told me he had gotten drunk a few times, with his brother Ted and his best friend Boots, when they were younger. "But I was living on my own at the time and was legally old enough to drink. I'd appreciate it if you'd show respect for the law as long as you're living in this house. I poured the beer out. Don't be late."

I wonder where I will be when Logan smokes his first cigarette or squirrels away some over-hyped copy of *Playboy,* sneaking breathless looks in the dim light of whatever hideaway he finds. Where will his secret place be? I won't smell his cigarette on a warm night, or find his bootleg stash by some quirk of happenstance. He won't know that I am aware of those parts of his life.

A few years ago, shortly before my parents sold the house in which we grew up, I went to visit them for a last look at the house, the back-yard, and the creek. My father had removed the tree house by then. One of the limbs supporting it had died, leaving the structure listing to one side, and he was afraid it would become a liability. But the rope swing was still there. I leaned against the rope, testing its strength against the weight of my body. Satisfied, I held tight to the rope and let gravity carry me far out over the creek. I looked up to the slowly spinning kaleidoscope of filtered sunlight, yellow-green leaves, and intersecting branches. How could he possibly have climbed up that near-vertical tree trunk, mostly bare of branches to use as hand- or footholds, in or-der to attach the swing? I could not imagine attempting that climb.

The image of my father perched nonchalantly in the upper limbs of that tree comes to me often since Logan's birth. I am awed by that im-age. I try, but cannot, to place myself as a father within the frame of that picture. I called my father recently to ask if I had it right in my mem-ory, and if so, how he had managed that impossible climb. His soft laugh bounced back through the phone line. "Don't you remember? I screwed iron pegs into the tree in a couple of places where there was no other hold; then I took the pegs out on my way down." He explained that it was a trick he learned when he worked during college as a line-man for a small electric company.

So now I see behind the image. My father, it turns out, is not super-human, not some kind of spider-man, but simply a good man wise enough to use the skills, knowledge, and tools at his disposal. Perhaps I should take comfort in this discovery and allow it to assuage my fears about long-distance fatherhood. Those fears are not easily set aside. Like landscape, relationships are shaped by both internal and external circumstances. My relationship with my father relied on steady contact and proximity. I rarely asked his advice directly, nor did he often offer it, but he knew, through continuous observation and contact, when I was veering off-course. And I knew there was little that escaped his quiet gaze. My model of fatherhood is a constant presence, quiet and gentle like a summer stream. I fear my reality as a father will be more like a desert wash, dry most of the time and then unable to contain the rush of water when it finally comes.

The thought of a desert wash daunts me, and yet I seek solace in another metaphor from the landscape I now inhabit. Though there are few flowing streams, and rainfall is infrequent, evidence of water is all around. Delicate paloverde trees burst up from the desert floor like green fountains. Giant saguaros expand like accordions to store a year's worth of water. Tough creosote bushes smell of rain even on the driest and hottest day. Surely there is a way, even without constant physical proximity, to give my son the quiet assurance I received from my father. It will not be the same, of course; it cannot. Nor will it be easy. My impulse is to fill our short and sporadic time together with as many experiences as possible; to rush from one thing to another, to explain myself so he will know who I am, and to pepper him with questions so I will know who he is. This is an impulse born of desperation. In my more lucid moments, I know the kind of relationship I want with him will not grow in that environment. And so I try to be patient, to allow us both to find our own course. Above all, I search for a way to reach through the distance to let him know I am here, watching and loving him. Some nights as I drift off to sleep, if the cool desert breeze is just right, I hear a faint but reassuring murmur coming, it seems, from somewhere beneath this dry landscape. It sounds like water.

The Unexpected

Near my fiftieth birthday I took off for a weekend in early spring to do some rambling. On an early Saturday morning I left Bellingham for Galiano Island, in the Gulf Islands of British Columbia. With dark skies, wind, and rain, the prospects looked bleak. But I had been postponing this trip for several months, for one reason or another—sickness, weather, family, or work—and time was running out.

The owner of a prospector's tent on a piece of land overlooking Active Pass was due back soon from Montreal. He had generously offered me as a solitary retreat his canvas abode, furnished with wood heat, a propane stove, and spring-fed running water. I had set the weekend before my birthday as a promise to myself, rain or no rain.

It takes an hour to drive from my house across the Canadian border to the Tsawwassen Ferry Terminal in British Columbia. At 7 A.M. there were no other waiting cars. I rolled my '85 Camry to a soft stop at the base of the checkpoint window, and waited to be questioned.

"Where do you live?"

"Planet Earth."

"Purpose of trip to Canada?"

"To contemplate my life at half century."

"Very good, sir, have a nice day," he said.

I left the Camry with the loud muffler, loose bushings, leaky head gasket, and vibrating distributor arm in long-term parking, and shouldering a daypack hurried toward the terminal. The wind was blowing hard from the southwest and momentarily took my breath away.

Because Galiano Island lies in the rain shadow cast by the Olympic Mountains across the Strait of Juan de Fuca, I was hoping for sunbreaks. When the ferry left the terminal at 8:40 A.M., the island was hidden in dense clouds, but after forty minutes of westerly travel, sunbreaks or "sucker holes" appeared, as promising and bright as the young children playing on the floor in the forward cabin.

The ferry docked briefly at the village of Sturdies Bay, at the south end of Galiano Island, and a few of us walked and drove off the boat. After walking through the small village, I took Burrill Road on the left and headed for "The Bluffs," a high point on the island on my way to my friend's property.

I passed many rustic houses with fruit trees and daffodil and crocus blooming in the yards, and small purple violets coloring the green grasses. Salmonberry, one of the first plants to bloom in the spring, was showy with its lovely pink flowers; ocean spray was leafing out, and large racemes drooped from the branches of big leaf maple.

I rambled along Burrill Road, generally following Active Pass between Galiano and Mayne Islands. Occasionally through a clearing I could see the water, and a boat or ferry moving toward, or returning from, Sydney or Victoria on Vancouver Island. I passed a house with a sign that read: "Billy's Eggs / Farm Fresh."

My father was called "Billy." Thoughts about my father go hand in hand with feelings for the land. He's a world-class gardener, but every opportunity he had he took me fishing or hunting. One of my earliest memories is feeling the pressure of his hand on mine as we waited to shoot squirrels from a large mulberry tree near his parents' home in southeastern Missouri. Because I was too small to hold the shotgun steady by myself, I rested the barrel on my father's shoulder while he put a finger in his ear to protect his eardrum from the blast. As I was growing up I frequently heard him say, "Had I been born a hundred years earlier, I would have been a mountain man."

As soon as I could hold a fishing pole, he had me fishing. One evening we were fishing in a floodplain along Big Creek, near Mudlick Mountain. I was probably five or six. It was getting dark, starting to drizzle, and the mosquitoes were ferocious. Father threw the line across the creek and the bait settled under the roots of an overhanging willow tree. He said he'd go get the minnow trap and come back in a few minutes. He handed me the pole and walked out of sight in his beat-up sneakers, squishing water with every step. I could hear him for a few minutes moving downstream, the gravel crunching underneath his feet, when a strong pull nearly ripped the rod from my hands. Like I'd been taught, I pulled back to set the hook. Soon my arms hurt badly, but I didn't let go of the pole. Just when I thought my arms were finished, I was able to drag a good-sized catfish up on the gravel bar where it flopped around for a couple minutes. I collapsed on the gravel bar, too, and lay there breathing deeply like the fish, for I had hooked into a power larger than myself. I liked the thrill of it.

When I was eleven years old, I purchased my first canoe, and my father and I took up canoeing. Some of my best memories from those
early teenage years are floating the clear, spring-fed Current River each
summer with my family. The summer I was sixteen, I learned canoe
camping during our first trip to the Boundary Waters Canoe Area in
northeastern Minnesota. During my twenties and thirties I worked for
Outward Bound all over North America and guided dozens of outdoor
adventures in the Appalachian and Cascade Mountains, in the Canadian bush, and through the canyon country of the American Southwest. The last outdoor adventure I guided was only six years ago. I've
been a model of consistency—which surely was put into motion by my
early experiences with the natural world that my father gave me.

Even though the skies were overcast, as I neared The Bluffs I decided to stop for lunch. I turned off the main road, now only one lane
and gravel, and walked a quarter mile to a sweeping and majestic view,
even under muted skies. There was a BC ferry moving up Active Pass,
against the westward flowing tide and current. The saltwater was
changing from high to low tide, and through binoculars I could see
the water surging through the channel between Galiano and Mayne Islands. The sky was spitting rain, but there were occasional sunbreaks—
typical of the dynamic spring weather in the Pacific Northwest—and
many of the Gulf Islands were visible. Directly to the south, across Active Pass, lay Mayne Island, and beyond—Saturna. Moving my binoculars slowly toward the west, I could see Pender, and in the misty, gray
distance Salt Spring Island.

I ate my lunch while sitting on a short Ensolite pad. A bald eagle, soaring nearby, dropped down for a closer look, landing in the
branches of a Douglas fir. The Bluffs were the high point of my walk
that day, at least literally. After lunch and rejoining the main road, I immediately began descending, past a small grove of old-growth cedar
trees—their lower branches, or withes, covered with moss. The road
I followed sloped away from The Bluffs toward a swamp.

The darkness of the interior forest changed the mood of my day, and
the flapping of large wings and the primeval call of a pileated wood-
pecker—balanced somewhere between hysterical crying and laughing—took my thoughts to my ten-year-old son, Noah.

Noah wakes me at 4 A.M. and crawls in next to me. "Stay home, stay
home," he says, "stay home, stay home, stay home."

"Don't worry, school will be fun," I say, hardly awake.

"Mrs. E is nice," he says, "stay home, stay home, stay home." He leans over and turns on the bedside lamp. "Get up, get up, get up, get up," he chants, the crescendo of demand increasing with each word.

As we head for the door, Noah turns with another request—"Pooh friends, Pooh friends." I shuffle into the next room where Noah has been sleeping with his mother and fetch Piglet, Rabbit, Tigger, and Pooh from the top of the pillow where he keeps them at night. I also grab two videos he has propped up against the wall. Susan pulls the covers up over her head.

Another day has begun—why didn't I go to bed earlier? On the way downstairs to the rec room, I grab a sweater and pair of socks for Noah, which I pull on him as one would any toddler.

Once downstairs he begins picking and sorting through his video collection that numbers well over a hundred. He finally picks one, but as I turn to go back upstairs, he grunts loudly to get my attention.

"Sit by you," he says.

"First, let me get you a snack," I say, and go back upstairs to the kitchen where I get him a tippy cup of orange juice and a bowl of Honey Nut Cheerios. I go back downstairs and sit by him; he's watching *Thomas the Tank Engine*. I soon begin to nod off. But he pulls on my arm: "New video, new video, new video," he says. We go through the process of choosing another one—shall it be Caillou, Maisey, Pooh Bear, Little Bill, Dora, Blues Clues, Rugrats, Barney, Little Bear, or a Walt Disney movie? After what feels like a very long time—at 4:30 in the morning—we settle in with another video, the *Tigger Movie*.

I look over at Noah. His eyes are lit up and he's laughing. He looks over at me when Tigger's in a jam—"Uh oh," he says, raising his arms in the air. "You can do it."

Noah's two front teeth are missing—like any young boy—and his hair is buzzed short for easy care. He looks typical, except perhaps for his ears, which are long and flat and don't have the usual curl at the top. He's also flapping his arms—like two large wings—in his enthrallment with the movie.

At 5 A.M. I begin to smell the familiar odor of BM. I wait until he's finished. "Noah, let's change your diaper."

He gets up and runs to the TV—"Rewind video, rewind, rewind, rewind," he yells.

"After I change your diaper," I say.

"Rewind, rewind, rewind." He wants to see the last episode again.

"Noah, let's change your diaper first."

"Rewind, rewind, rewind." I give in and push the rewind button. Noah squeals with pleasure.

I go to the bathroom and get a towel, baby wipes, powder, and Desitin ointment in case he has a diaper rash. I guide him down to the towel on the floor and pull off his socks and pajama shorts. I undo the diaper and clean him as best I can:

> With warm water
> I wash his ten-year-old bottom, flaming red.
> I could kiss his red butt hole
> I am so close.

It's 5:30 A.M. Noah wants a snack. Back upstairs for buttered bread, cheese, apple, and soy milk—the staples of his diet. He eats with relish, smiling up at me with full mouth. But now he no longer wants to watch the video, asking for "Disney Channel" instead. For the next hour or so we alternate between TV shows and videos until the rest of the family is heard upstairs—7 A.M. and time for breakfast.

When Noah was fifteen months old, our pediatrician started thinking that he wasn't developing normally. Noah wasn't talking or walking, and when he got excited he would flap his arms rapidly like a happy, strange bird. It was such a funny gesture. In a desire to solve the mystery, our pediatrician urged us to see this or that specialist. After several months of fruitless testing, a neurologist discovered that Noah has fragile X syndrome, the most common inherited cause of mental retardation.

My wife, Susan, carries the genetic code in her DNA that includes fragile X. Because this is the first incident of fragile X in either family, we learned through genetic counseling that at the time of Susan's conception there was probably a mutation on one of her X chromosomes, which she passed to Noah. Because boys have only one X chromosome (and one Y chromosome), they are usually more impacted than girls (who have two X chromosomes).

Fragile X is caused by a central nervous system dysfunction, and the range of affliction can run from mild to severe. Noah is now ten years old, and it is evident that he is severely affected. Outwardly, Noah looks like a typical fourth grader, standing over four feet tall and weighing seventy pounds, but he's still too timid to get into a canoe, or any boat floating on water for that matter. (By the time I was his age, I had a paper route and was saving up for my first canoe.)

He's afraid of the smallest heights, and when he accompanies me to the library I have to carry him down the stairs. He can't ride a bike, dress himself, or tie his shoes. He prefers his fingers to eating utensils. Though he can walk short distances, he has many developmental delays that keep him from the outdoor activities that I love to do.

Funny how life works out. There were a couple of women I almost married before I met Susan. I can't help but wonder about the physical and moral laws of Nature that brought my son to me. I love him more than I can say, but sometimes I feel sorry for myself, and frustrated—that I can't do the typical outdoor things that a father does with his son.

When we first found out that Noah had fragile X, it was like an earthquake or tornado had suddenly swept away the foundations of our lives. But we eventually recovered and went through a normal grieving period, denial, and then gradually acceptance. When I began to tell my friends, family, and associates about Noah, to a person they would be sympathetic and offer kind words of condolence—similar to what you say to a colleague who unexpectedly loses a parent or family member.

After a week of school, Noah likes to spend his Saturday in front of the TV. His idea of an outdoor activity is going to Kmart or Target to look at videos. Although these stores are anathemas to me, I usually comply with such activities because they make my son happy.

For each video he considers, he sticks it in his mouth. He begins cooing and flapping his arms. He grabs video box after video box, and after tasting them fondles them in his hands. Within a few minutes his gurgling and lack of speech for a boy so large has attracted the attention of the other shoppers.

After forty-five minutes of checking and tasting, it's time to go; I buy a video to get us peaceably out of the store.

On Sunday I take Noah for a walk to the neighborhood park. After much protesting from him, I get him outside. But he insists we take his "Pooh friends" and use the "jogger"—a special stroller made for him.

At the park he gets out of the jogger and wants to play hide and seek, and later Billy-Goat Gruff, where I pretend I'm a troll. Thirty to forty minutes of fun toddler play. But then he falls apart—flings his Pooh friends into the bushes—for no explicable reason. A tantrum. He refuses to walk or get into the jogger. He screams, he hits me in the face.

Though he plays like a toddler, he hits like a ten-year-old.

Everyone else is watching now. I manhandle him into the jogger, protecting myself as best as I can from the kicking, hitting, biting.

Back home, I put on a video, change his wet diaper, give him a snack, and he mellows. Later, he's hugging me and wanting to wrestle on the floor.

I have many Native American friends, Navajos from when I taught in the American Southwest and Salish who live in western Washington. Gradually, when they asked in conversation about my two children, I would explain to them about Noah. What a difference in their responses: "What a gift," they would say; or, "What a blessing!"

The first time I heard this my face must have betrayed my surprise, because my Salish friend began to explain. "In our culture," he told me, "a child like Noah is seen as a spiritual teacher. If your heart is open, he will teach you a great deal about yourself and what it means to be human."

I've often thought about the responses to Noah from my Native friends. Thirty years ago and beyond, children like Noah would typically have been institutionalized, separated from mainstream culture. Because of this, their life span was usually only thirty to forty years. Today, we don't as frequently hide or put away atypical people. But emotionally, when confronted with someone with different abilities and special needs, we still tend to react with confusion and fear to what Nature has wrought.

It's like avoiding the effects of an oncoming hurricane. We try to remove outselves from its path as quickly as possible. But to live daily with these winds, to accept them, to love them, is what my Native friends are encouraging me to do. Although I typically identify with what I perceive as positive, and shun what I perceive as negative, I need to contemplate both sides of the coin in order to reestablish harmony and balance with what I call Nature. Because Noah is my son, and because I am trying to be the best father I can be, Noah has enabled me to come to terms with attributes of Nature that I never could have without him.

I think these thoughts as the road I'm following leaves the cedar swamp and reenters open country bordering Active Pass. The recent squall has passed and the island country is now flooded in golden sunlight. Several winter wrens I can't see, hiding in the nearby ferns and underbrush, let loose with a delightful, melodic chorus.

My coming of age during the Vietnam War was a difficult experience for my father and me. We fought a lot about politics, curfews, girls, cars, drugs, and religion. But we both found solace in the out-of-doors. He hunted and fished; I was into rock climbing, backpacking, and canoeing.

My father's best friend had a small A-frame cabin in the woods bordering Shawnee National Forest in southern Illinois. We often went there together during my teenage years. In 1970 when I was eighteen years old, I went there alone, for fourteen days, to consider where my life was going, or not going. Getting away occasionally, to be alone, naturally, with myself, is something I've kept doing on a regular basis since that time.

As I head toward my friend's piece of island, accessible only by trail or water, I consider another twist in the father-son relationship. Under my father's tutelage I learned much about the commonly revered attributes of Nature. But every day my son gives me an opportunity to fathom sublimity in the paradoxes of his disability, in what appears on the surface to be wanton and destructive.

> My wife's waters broke in bed.
> We were lying side-by-side,
> On wet, white sheets.
>
> Eighteen months later, I was as surprised as anyone
> To learn my son was mentally retarded—
> Should I use the word impaired?
> Disabled?
> What you call it doesn't matter,
> Except when trying to explain.

Hellgrammite Dance

We found you under a rock.

That was my father's consistent answer whenever I asked him how I came to be. As a young boy—when we still lived in Missoula—I imagined my parents lifting and rolling over a deeply embedded rock in some open Montana hillside filled with huckleberry bushes or beargrass, like two bears looking for grub. Later—after we had moved to Los Angeles in an old Chevy during the summer of 1968—the rock I imagined my parents turning over was usually in the desert, like some miniature Vasquez, scorpions scuttering away at the movement. There I would be, exposed, hauled out of that cool darkness to begin a new life, light blinding my eyes.

I was named after an old Navy buddy of my father's, my parents tell me, but I have never quite believed it so accidental that they gave me the name Stanley—stone lea, rocky place where the light shines, stony meadow.

3 July 1997, Caldwell—Yesterday, Arwen, Ruth, and I drew a pictorial map of our neighborhood, including Sacajawea Elementary, the cemetery, Boise River, the hill, and our blue house and yard. Ruth drew Arwen and herself swinging on pink swings next to the house. Arwen drew a horse. Then Ruth asked for the butterfly field guide and began playing school with it. She told me her teacher was Arwen Swallowtail. Later, on a picnic to Canyon Hill Cemetery, we found a marble bench with "Oregon Trail 1844–65" engraved on it. I told the girls stories about the Oregon Trail and the people who came through here, including the boy who drowned in the river. Arwen and Ruth like to visit the part of the cemetery where all the children are buried, walking among the photos, stuffed animals, and pinwheels keeling sideways. How old was this girl, this boy, this baby, they ask me. Then Arwen asks how babies are made. So I tell her and Ruth, too. Our first discussion of sex, right there among the gravestones under the big shade trees along the cliff edge of the cemetery. I wonder what they will remember.

The first time I remember my father telling me about sex, he was working on the engine of his Volkswagen van, sitting on the curb, hands black and greasy, not really looking at me, but explaining all the details. Perhaps he had been spurred on by his discovery of all the pictures of nude women I had stuffed down beside the mattress I slept on in the unfinished room upstairs. I was thirteen years old at the time, and had come north to Tacoma from LA with my younger brother and sister to spend a month with my father during the summer.

We spent much of the summer in the backyard, under the enormous madrone playing badminton and croquet. Our croquet courses required sending the balls over thick roots and going behind the covered sandbox—the more obstacles the better. On hot days my father put the hose into the sandbox; we made a sandy mountain, inserted the hose into it, and then turned it on. Slowly the top of the mountain would bulge and shift, the pressure building, and then, suddenly, the water would pour down the mountainside, all of us fascinated by the stream-making patterns of erosion.

That summer something had been changing in my body, too. Something had eroded, some mountain had finally given way to the building pressure, the urges, the desire, the release.

25 October 1997, Bellingham—How to explore eros and mountains, the "procreant urge" (as Whitman put it) and subducting continental plates, one's own body and the body of the earth? Certainly others have suggested the erotic possibilities of mountains—think of the Tetons, or the sensual paintings of buttes by O'Keeffe. Mountains rise toward a vertical landscape, humans walk upright. We notice them because they are like us.—Ruth asks me what I am writing about. Mountains, I say. Oh, she says, like Mt. Baker? Mt. Rainier? or Mt. Everest? Yes, I say. Then she shows me where she bit off her chocolate graham cracker. There's a mountain, she says.

> *What is a mountain, asked the child as we sat on a flat stone on the side*
> *   of the trail, her breath heavy, mine deep and steady,*
> *What could I tell her? Doesn't she know as well as I?*
> *Perhaps it is the inversion of space, the humped back of a whale rising*
> *   above the waves.*
> *Ruth: a hill, a climbing thing, a mountain is a mountain, a tennis shoe*
> *   place because there is rocks and snow.*
> *Why is a mountain there? They grew, says Ruth.*

Fathering has come to this: one day I am comfortably making maps of the neighborhood, imagining swallowtails as teachers, the next day picnicking in a cemetery marked by the lives and deaths of nineteenth-century overland travelers, and then suddenly trying to explain for the first time to my seven- and four-year-old daughters how babies are made, how all of this began, our bodies, life, consciousness, these mysteries of existence and death.

When Sylvia was five months pregnant with Arwen, our first child, I received a letter from my father—two pages, typed single-spaced like all his letters on an old manual Smith Corona, rows of pound signs crossing out words and phrases:

Now you are ready to enter this world wherein you will learn through on the job training. All your prior perceptions of what it will mean, what you will do, and how you will deal with it will be altered by the reality of that little person who quickly exerts a mind of their own. Most everything in our world can become a loss in our life, but parenthood seems to linger forever. My mom still worries about me as I do her, and in a sense we both still adjust our lives a little for each other. And I look at my own life and the five of you kids who have become even more as you leave home, marry, and have your own families. . . . As I think of you right now all sorts of pictures flash across my memory and they are good memories, memories of joy, of pride, of love. I know there were times when I wasn't there for you, times when my own needs were first, times when I wondered why I even had kids or got married as I struggled to make a living, and these will be a part of your own life, but . . . all this guilt that I carry is put in perspective by your open and continual love of me. To know that parenthood is not perfect makes it something we ordinary people can enjoy and struggle with. I tell all my students that to have a child is a tremendous act of faith, as the world can turn that act into pain so many ways. If a person wants something cute in their lives they should get a puppy, if they want a force that will change their lives, they should have kids.

For nearly twelve years our lives have been changing in a direction I can barely decipher, on a trajectory that is as mysterious to me as my own existence. How is it, I wonder, that stardust has coalesced into such exquisite and complicated lives as my own, my daughters', my father's, yours? When does any particular life ever begin? In the moment of conception? In the emergence from seed, earth, egg, womb? In some long time frame of evolutionary processes? In the mind of the Creator? Or is it somewhere in our imagining? And what does it mean, I wonder, to have a father and two daughters? What happens to all the connections between our lives when we die?

22 September 1996, Jordan Craters—
When a great-horned owl flies
up and out of the lava tube rattling
the breath from our lungs, Arwen rushes to the edge
my fear for her nearly overwhelming
her desire to gaze into this black hole.

Being a son and a father has meant living in the fluidity of time and place. I say something to Arwen and hear my father speaking to me years ago. I walk over river stones with my father on a fishing trip up the Beckler River and think of me and Ruth hopping rocks all the way up to the source of a stream in the Adirondacks. These moments of time, and the memories in each of these places, flow into and out of each other. Any one of the particular events in this essay could be its own story, but it doesn't seem right to separate them. The voices that speak from these disjointed journal entries, letters, memories, and relationships—which weave themselves into new patterns and juxtapositions every day—have been pieced together like this because this is what my life has been like as a child and parent.

My journals are full of unanswered questions, poem fragments, sketches, and reflections from my life. Scattered between are observations on my daughters' lives, which puzzle me; they read like a mere reporting of events. What these journal entries might mean about who Arwen and Ruth are, who they are becoming, what such events say about my own fathering, or even what it is that Arwen and Ruth will remember, I hardly know. I keep on writing—and fathering—anyway, hoping that somehow all of these fragments from our lives, mine and theirs, are coming together into something whole.

Only now, as a father, am I beginning to understand some of the ways my father shaped me when I was a child and a young man. There were magical times we spent together on rivers fishing and exploring. There were long periods of his absence after he and my mother divorced two years after we moved to LA. There were also his letters, which came to me often as gifts, each one eventually bundled with the others and hauled from place to place like some kind of sacred text to be savored again and again. And in the last twenty years we have come to know each other as adults, as teachers, and as fathers. At the end of that letter my father wrote to me just before Arwen was born, he added: *Last night I had a huckleberry milkshake which gave me a rush of*

thoughts about the West Fork last summer and watching the joy and deter-
mination of Sylvia as she became a part of the Bitterroot gang.

During the summer Arwen is conceived, Sylvia and I come to western Montana to see my extended family and to experience what I love most about the place I still consider my homeground: cold, trout-filled rivers and huckleberries. We have been married four years, living in Iowa for the last three, and this summer have been eager to leave the heat and humidity of the Midwest for the dry warmth of the northern Rockies. We are also ready to become parents for the first time. For several days we stay at my uncle and aunt's cabin on the Clark Fork River, swimming, canoeing, and lounging around. When I ask my aunt about good places to go huckleberry picking, she directs us toward a patch she has seen miles up a logging road on the auspiciously named Sex Peak.

In my family, huckleberry picking has always been done by women and children. The men would usually go off fighting forest fires, drinking beer, driving their boats on the lake, or fishing. Though I remember a few of those trips with the men to Seeley Lake to pick up a case of Lucky Lager, nothing compares to the intensity of my memories of picking huckleberries way out on the edges of some logging road with my sister, my mother, aunts, and my grandmother, my mother's mother, who once held her ground against a bear in a huckleberry patch. She and the bear kept picking, neither giving way. I like to think they had a mutual respect for each other: both knew the value of a good patch of huckleberries. We would come home with our containers full and put the purple berries in homemade vanilla ice cream and pancakes, and make huckleberry jam.

The patch we find on Sex Peak is thick with berries, and several steaming bear scat piles mark the side of the road. I head up the hill, picking all the way, and Sylvia, sensibly, picks berries closer to the car, her eyes on the lookout for large hairy movements through the bushes. We see no bears, but fill our containers and stomachs—our lips and fingers purple—and then return again the next day. Days later we stand in the Missoula kitchen of my other grandmother, my father's mother, cooking our huckleberries into the liquidy tart jam my father later uses to make his milkshake.

25 July 1994, Boundary Waters—This evening I took Ruth on a short canoe
excursion to "Blueberry Island"—so named for its abundance of ripe berries

on top. A loon sat on its nest by the water, its mate swimming in the lake nearby. We scrambled up the rocks, Ruthie clinging to me. On top I set her down among the blueberries and she just started picking and eating. She picks mostly ripe berries, but occasionally eats a green one too. She also discovered the raspberries near camp.

31 July 1996, Paradise Point—Arwen is wading in the lake after a full morning of drawing and painting. Few clouds this morning—the air hazy above the ridge-lines. Arwen and I picked huckleberries again on the red-dot trail—the bushes wet and soaking our shoes and jeans. Arwen would stop picking and seem to meditate, or listen intently, or just remain quiet in waist-high huckleberry bushes. Yesterday she asked me about bears coming, today she heard noises—steps, she said. Then two deer appeared—white rumps, curious about us, walking slowly through the woods. Squirrels overhead were nipping cones and the cones falling all around, sometimes within ten feet or so—the dangers of huckleberrying.

After the jam has cooled in the jars, my father arrives in Missoula, where we are sleeping upstairs in one of the tiny hot bedrooms of my grandmother's house, the mattress on the bed so springy and noisy that we have to put it on the floor to get any sleep at all. My father grew up in this house with his two brothers. His father, Woldemar—or Walt, as everyone called him—repaired shoes, grew gorgeous flowers, smoked cigars, and loved to fish. One of my favorite photographs of myself is one Grandpa took of me holding a string of trout—my head is cut off because, as usual, he just aimed the camera without really looking into it. I remember walking with him in the wet grass in the dark in the backyard of that house, flashlight in hand, looking for nightcrawlers, pulling their slick-skinned bodies from the grass and putting them in a coffee can for the next day's fishing trip to the West Fork or the Big Blackfoot.

Grandpa died when I was ten, and ten years later I wrote a poem called "Angles," a poem that remembers Walt

> *standing thigh-deep in the Blackfoot,*
> *smoking his cigar*
> *losing smoke curls in whirlpools*
> *spun between his legs.*

That poem helped to change my relationship to my father, opening up for us, through poetry, a river of words to speak about the powerful emotional connections between a son, his father, and his father's father. The fall before I wrote "Angles," my mother's father, Dean, had died in Spokane, where I was attending college. His death came suddenly and set me to writing poetry for the first time, to somehow express the inexpressible feelings I had about him. After the memorial service, a letter arrived from my father:

I'm sorry he couldn't have enjoyed a longer and more joyful life. That thing that happened to me last fall set me a thinking about what my death would mean and I sort of decided that if it happens right now I can rightfully say that my life has been full, exciting, full of wonderment, satisfying, frustrating, loving, and above all worth it. All sorts of ideas and beliefs have been put forward about after death and I suppose all have some validity and meaning, but I choose to believe that death is the end, and then for the person who has died nothing exists. I do not see that in any cynical way, but only as the logical outgrowth of my own epistemology. To me, nothing after death is simple, all-encompassing, a fitting end for one small part of the life that exists in this universe. Man spends too much time methinks exalting his place in the family of living creatures. My focus is away from death as something meaningful to life and the quality of life. . . . What I hope is that when death stops my life, you will all celebrate the fact that life for me has so much worth and that you and the rest of the kids were and are a great part of that. I guess there are so many things to fear beside death.

The Bitterroot Gang—as my father calls us—heads south from Missoula on Highway 93 to fish the West Fork of the Bitterroot River, a route as familiar to me as any. I cannot remember the first time my father took me fishing on the West Fork, for the memories all slide together. Sometimes we are climbing through barbed-wire fences along the edges of fields, trying not to snag our lines behind us. Sometimes stepping into the river before the sun has come up, my feet wet and cold in old tennis shoes. Or catching grasshoppers in the tall grass next to the river—patiently stalking, each movement slow and steady, and then the cupped-hand pounce, those long legs tickling my palm. Or gorging ourselves on ripe raspberries growing on a rocky island in the middle of the river.

In my earliest memories, my father carries his old creel over his shoulder stuffed with freshly torn grass for the swiftly caught cutthroat trout. And he is smoking his pipe, Flying Dutchman tobacco burning swirls into the air above us. On the river he shows me where the trout are, how the water moves, where to cast, and how to see what is beneath the surface. I want Sylvia to experience something of this magic I have always felt on this river, and to make some of our own memories to take with us back to Iowa.

On Sundays, when my father was a kid, his parents would take him and his brothers up Nine Mile or Lolo Creek for a picnic and some fishing. Sometimes, after a meal, Grandpa would fish the stream with his nightcrawlers, smoking his cigar, and Grandma would get the boys into the water, downstream, building a dam. Once, as they pulled up the rocks, strange-looking water critters swirled up to the surface. My father had always loved bugs. When he grabbed some of the black scaly creatures that looked like fat prehistoric dragonflies with no wings and took them to his father, Grandpa told him those were hellgrammites.

Grandpa always used nightcrawlers to fish, but my father and his brothers starting catching these hellgrammites, and soon discovered how eager the trout were to strike a fat, black, squirming hellgrammite on a hook, especially just before the stonefly hatch. A hellgrammite is a naiad that lives under the rocks in the swift part of a stream, and later, at the designated time, crawls out of the water onto a rock or tree and stops there; its outer skin then slowly cracks apart, and an adult stonefly hatches out of the dried skin into its brief life of frenzied mating, laying of eggs, and death.

25 August 1997, Bayview State Park—After we set up camp yesterday, Ruth and I went for a walk down the beach—beachcombing. At first Ruth just wanted to walk, but then as we slowed down we found pieces of clam shells, and fragments of crabs. We also found part of an oyster shell and a few whole clams. We found two dead birds, one in the seaweed, tangled up, with whitish feathers underneath, the other a dark bird with red feet. It was lying on the rocks, its neck twisted, right in front of where we stopped to eat. We talked about the bugs eating the bird and us eating our salami and bread—how living things eat dead things, how everything that lives will eventually die, how dead things nourish, give strength to, and enable living things to continue to live. Ruth had many questions about life and death. She kept asking whether the dead birds were "mama birds."

The first order of business on a fishing trip to the West Fork is to find a good stretch of river to collect hellgrammites, a place where the water rushes swiftly over a wide bed of rocks. When we stop the truck, my father pulls out his homemade hellgrammite net—a wire screen nailed like a scroll between two 2-by-2s—and steps into the water. My uncle follows, taking a position upstream from my father, who is now holding the net down in the water, and begins what we call the hellgrammite dance. The person upstream—the dancer—has to wedge feet down under the rocks, and flick them, roll them, move them, disturb them in any way possible so that all the creatures living below the rocks are swept out and onto the hellgrammite net downstream. Depending upon your perspective, the dancer's movement may look comical or ritualistic: arms flailing to keep the body's balance on the slippery stones, legs rocking and rolling like an awkward dancing partner. *Dip, churn, stumble, sway.* Eventually, the net-holder signals the dancer to stop and lifts the screen above the surface of the river, the dancer now swiftly grabbing the largest black hellgrammites scurrying over each other. There are also tiny red worms, caddisfly larvae, a small bullfish, and other river-bottom creatures and debris scattered over the net. The hellgrammites are placed in containers filled with water and punched with air holes to keep them as fresh as possible.

My father calls me out into the river to take my uncle's place. At first, as I stumble through the icy water, I feel like some clumsy Godzilla upturning the river homes at my feet, but then I begin to nudge my toes down under rocks, pushing them around, feeling the rhythm of the current. As I dance the river clouds up below me, and I hear laughter from the riverbank. I can feel the power of the water eroding some mountain inside me, and the quick release of all those lives huddled under the stones. Enough, says my father, lifting the net out of the water. I pick the skittery hellgrammites from the net and wonder about their watery lives—their three-year journey from eggs to naiads to adults, molting several times along the way—and the cutthroat trout they will feed and fatten, and the people like us who will catch and eat the trout. When I walk back to the riverbank, my old, blue Flying Dutchman tobacco can is stuffed with hellgrammites. I hold the can up, and Sylvia and I hear the hellgrammite legs scratching the metal inside. They want to live. So do we.

On my twenty-second birthday, I received a letter from my father:

The dafs are coming up all around here and spring is on the way and I sort of feel like them as I poke my head out of all the winter complications and look at doing some new things this year. . . . Some of the pondering I have been doing lately comes from the fact that I have grown tired of being part of the 105 *endless lies. I want some cold hard truth to raise its ugly but compelling head. I'm not sure what I really mean by truth but I know it is not universal, or complete, or enlightening, and comfortable; but it is refreshing. Life is worth more than we say. Quality is greater than quantity. We surround ourselves with all types of expressions that confuse, that hide our true feelings, that give us the illusion that we are civilized, yet at the same time we kill, and plunder, and hurt so many. This endless paradox in human actions and slogans leads me close to a clearer understanding of why I believe that all there is is what exists. There is nothing after life, there is no universal order, there is nothing except ourselves trying to make our way through an ever-changing set of situations that we have only a little power to shape or understand. That may sound very cold and godless to some, but to me this narrow and finite view of man gives me a type of optimism that sustains me as I am endlessly bombarded by man's crazy actions.*

Near the end of the letter, he talks about how exciting it is to see his children lose their innocence and to grow up, but also, as a parent, how much more complicated and harder it is to make right those things that confront his children.

I know more now that I don't look at you all becoming adults as a going away, but as a continuous progression in my own life as I rediscover you all again. Like the thought of fishing together this spring or whatever we do. And that is important to know—we need to take those times together and make the most of them and not fall into the old pattern of parent and child, but of two people who love each other and who need to express it as well as open ourselves to the other's inner thoughts and life.

One day Arwen and I were walking through the cemetery up on the hill near our home in Caldwell, reading gravestones and watching the osprey soar out over the Boise River below us. She asked me where I wanted to be buried when I die. I told her that I didn't want to be buried, but cremated. What did that mean, she asked. To be burned up until I became ashes. Then, I told her, my ashes could be scattered in the woods on some mountainside, or perhaps in a river, settling beneath the rocks. She didn't say anything more about it that day. We watched a blue heron standing below us in the stillness of an irrigation canal that feeds the river, both of us rapt, silent. The next day, when Arwen climbed out of bed, she said that if my ashes were spread in the woods, she could go there, and walk through the trees, and think about me.

15 August 2000, Big Heart Lake — On hectic days in the fall at school, at home, I want to think about this lake, remember the cool breeze on my ears, cheeks, chin; remember Ruth and Arwen casting their light lines out in arcs across the dark, cold lake; remember the sound of water flowing out of the lake and down over granite; remember the silence of the snow patches up on the mountain across from the lake; remember the "eeeeep" "eeeeep" of the pikas.

> *On the map, Ruth said, the lake*
> *did not look like a heart.*
> *One side is squished. But here*
> *at the lake's edge, huddling on granite*
> *behind white-gray deadfall, a pile*
> *of disintegrating trees*
> *holds the lake back momentarily*
> *for frogs, small fry, and moss —*
> *the wind coming straight off ice sheets*
> *between spindly trees clinging to rock.*
> *I wonder what makes a heart big,*
> *what beats louder than the silence*
> *of these waters.*

Arwen was born in May of 1990. My father counted back nine months to the previous August and our trip to Montana. It was the hellgrammite dance that did it, he declared, delighted in this revelation. The rocks we had stirred up in the West Fork had released something powerful into the world, a force that would change our lives: a daughter.

Now we have two. As they grow up, Ruth and Arwen keep asking — in new ways — how they came to be. Sometimes I am tempted to offer them a smart-aleck response like my father's — *We found you under a rock* — something they may ponder, as I have, for thirty years or more. Usually I take them outside, to the mountains, the ocean, forests, and rivers, and we play and explore, keep journals, and talk about it all.

In spite of my own vivid imagination, my parents have never been bears, nor desert scavengers, but common river folk — born themselves along the banks of rivers, Clark Fork and Spokane, that feed the vast Columbia River watershed. If they found me under a rock at all, it must have been a river rock. There I would be, like some hellgrammite waiting for the right moment to emerge from water to air, hauled out of that cool darkness to begin a new life, light blinding my eyes. So, to the rock in the Montana meadow and the rock in the California desert, I add this rock, which I now know has been there all along, resting under the water in the cold and swift trout-filled river of my heart.

16 August 2000, Big Heart Lake—Yesterday, a moment down by the river, putting my feet in the cold water, Sylvia coming to sit by me on the log, then Arwen, then Ruth—all of us huddled there in the cool wind, then Arwen taking off her sandals and hesitating to put her feet in the water, Sylvia saying who could keep their feet in the longest, so Arwen and I plunge ours in, skin numbing past the point that really matters—we could go on like this for a long time I think—Arwen, too. Then I finally pull my feet up and Arwen is delighted to win. Later her feet begin to tingle with needle-like pain as they thaw and warm.

At the very end of the letter my father sent me on my twenty-second birthday, he concludes:

I think all of this I have written is sort of like the dafs that I mentioned in the first. They push their heads up out of the dirt knowing all so well that the moment of flowering will be brief and dangerous. . . . I am trying to look at things with new life, trying to throw off some of the constraints I put on myself, and to struggle toward what I feel is the truth. I suppose I want to feel the joy of discovery. . . . Joy and quality—so worth the struggle. Happy birthday Stan. I love you and let us work hard to make good times happen for us. For sure I will see you in April.

In his words I can still feel my fishing pole bending above my head, curving like the daffodils' yellow petals that signal the beginning of spring, my father standing next to me, both of us watching the stoneflies hatching over the river. Maybe it will happen again next summer, this time with Arwen and Ruth. We will all head across the mountains to Montana and the West Fork, our hellgrammite net and fishing poles in hand, and look under the rocks in the river, seeing what we can stir up. Whether my father makes it or not, though, his words are already rocks on the riverbed, each one stirring the water that flows through me into life-giving riffles. I am eager to see how Arwen and Ruth will enter the river themselves, and dance their own hellgrammite dances. *Dip, churn, swirl, and sway. Dip, turn, stone, fly away.*

FATHERING

Eating Dirt

I have a small daughter and two smaller sons, twins. They are all three
in our minuscule garden at the moment, my sons eating dirt as fast as
they can get it off the planet and down their gullets. They are two years
old, they were seized with dirt-fever an instant ago, and as admirably
direct and forceful young men, quick to act, true sons of the West, they
are going to *eat some dirt*, boy, and you'd better step aside.

My daughter and I step aside.

The boys are eating so much dirt so fast that much of it is missing
their maws and sliding muddily down their chicken chests. It is thick
moist dirt, slightly more solid than liquid. I watch a handful as it travels toward the sun. It's rich brown stuff, almost black, crumbly. There
are a couple of tiny pebbles, the thin lacy bones of a former leaf (alder?
hawthorn?), the end of a worm, the tiny green elbows of bean sprouts.
In a moment I will pull the boy over and issue a ticket and a stern
speech about eating beans before their time, but right now I watch
with interest as he inserts the dirt, chews meditatively, emits the wrig-
gling worm, stares at it—and eats it again.

"Dad, they're *eating the garden*," says my daughter.

So they are. I'll stop them soon, before they eat more of the world
than they should, but for this rare minute in life we are all absorbed by
dirt, our faces to the ground, and I feel, inarticulately, that there's
something simple and true going on here, some lesson they should absorb, and so I let them absorb dirt.

It occurs to me that we all eat dirt. Fruits and vegetables are dirt
transformed by light and water. Animals are vigorous dirt, having
dined on fruit or vegetables or other animals who dine on flora. Our
houses and schools and offices are cupped by dirt and made of wood
and stone and brick—former dirt. Glass is largely melted sand, a kind
of clean dirt. Our clothing used to be dirt. Paper was trees was dirt. We
shape dirt into pots, plates, mugs, vases. We breathe dirt suspended
in the air, we crunch it between our teeth on spinach leaves and fresh
carrots, we wear it in the lines of our hands and the folds of our faces,

we catch it in the linings of our noses and eyes and ears. Some people are driven by private fires to eat dirt, often during pregnancy—the condition is called *pica*, from the Latin word for magpie.

In short we swim in an ocean of dirt, yet we hardly ever consider it closely, except to plumb it for its treasures, or furrow it for seed, or banish it from our persons, clothes, houses. We're suckers for *dramatic* former dirt—cougars, lilies, bears, redwoods—but don't often reflect on the basic stuff itself: good old simple regular normal orthodox there-it-sits-under-everything dirt.

My sons, filled with fill, turn their attentions to the other denizens of the garden: bamboo, beetles, blackberry, carrots, dockweed, cedars, camellias, dandelions, garlic, hawthorn, jays, moles, shrews, slugs, snails, spiders, squirrels—all made of dirt, directly or indirectly.

I am hardly handy about the house and garden, and spend my hours on other matters, but enough of me feels responsible for the dirt that surrounds my home that I have often regretted the general reckless abandonment of my garden, and felt a certain guilt that it is not productive, that the land lies fallow, that little food for our table grows there. But now, sitting against the old fence, cradling my daughter, grinning at the mud monkeys, I see that the garden is *itself* hard at work, hatching honey ants and potato bugs, propelling bamboo and beans into the air, serving as a grocery store for shrews. I imagine it in one of those sped-up film clips, madly roiling with animals and plants, the sun and rain baking and hammering it at a terrific pace, the banks of clouds sliding over like vast battleships.

Such busy dirt.

The children tire, the sun retreats, in we go to baths and beds. I wash the garden off my sons. It swirls down the bath-drain, into the river, eventually to the ocean. So some of my garden ends up as silt, some sinks to the ocean floor, some becomes kelp and razor clams and sea otters, some is drawn up again into rain; and maybe some returns to the garden, after a nearly unimaginable vacation.

My daughter and I discuss the journeys of dirt. And when the rain begins that evening, the first of the rains that define fall and winter here, she and I draw a map for our dirt, so that it will know how to come home to our house, and we leave the map on the back porch for the dirt to read.

"Maybe there are dirt fairies," says my daughter. "Or maybe the dirt can read. Who knows?"

Maybe my daughter—named for a flower that flows up from the

dirt with extraordinary thin-necked elegance and lift—is right about this. Maybe the dirt *can* read. Certainly, in a very real sense, the dirt can write: Consider, for example, this essay, made by dirt worked in wondrous ways into bone, blood, protein, water, and electricity. So dirt leans against a fence with lovely dirt in his lap, and watches dirt demons devour dirt, and the world spins in its miraculous mysterious circles, dust unto dust.

Such busy dirt, such a blizzard of blessings.

Loving Homer

It is early evening on the farm when Emma, her mother, and I take a final walk around the pond before going indoors. Sunset is turning the beardgrass crimson and darkening the volcanic hills nearby; their silhouettes are shaped like enormous haystacks on the horizon. Reluctant to stop browsing, the goats are bleating and muttering as they slowly abandon their grassy paddock for the security of the barn. Their bells jangle, then fall silent. Beyond the goats' shelter, our donkey, Magnolia, will graze all night. We can barely see her now, still feeding in the robust kikuyu in the lower pasture. Lisa and I try to hold on to twilights like this one as long as possible, when the afternoon heat has lifted, the animals have settled down, and the frogs have begun their desirous conversations with one another across the pond. Nearly three years old, Emma is ambling along the path behind us, lost in her own thoughts.

All at once, a small, winged shadow flashes across the sky, just above our heads. "Bats!" Emma shouts, delighted. In an instant, the little shadow is gone and there are only faint stars. Lisa and I exchange a disappointed look: no, we indicate wordlessly to each other; it was more likely a bird, hurrying to its nest before the sun sets completely; the flight path was too straight, the wing-beat too regular. Besides, we haven't seen bats all summer.

Later, over dinner, the two of us talk about what Emma might have been naming at the pond. Her mind-tools are different from ours. Her responses to things she sees take unpredictable zigzags, now that she's on the cusp between thinking with her whole body and thinking mostly with language—though of course she will use both modes to some degree all her life. For now, Emma's perceptions, emotions, and actions are often blurred together as she reacts to the world's plenitude of phenomena. She's growing into being a language-using creature, and in a few more years literacy's influence will be on her with full force. In the meantime, her communication is complex, creative, and in certain ways more winged and eloquent than it will ever be again.

Had Emma really meant to name a specific animal? It has been months since we've seen any bats. What was she remembering? Perhaps an evening in December when darting, birdlike shadows had whirled overhead and Lisa and I had called to her in our excitement, "Look! Bats!" In that moment, as she'd spun around, trying to look where we were pointing, what had that word come to mean for her? Perhaps a cool twilight, the night's first stars reflected in the pond, the crying of a bird, her father and mother holding hands, and then a fluttering that had parted the air and startled us into giving her a word for all of this.

Out of habit tonight, we had taken Emma's "bats!" to be the naming of something that was only part of our sunset walk—something whose identity we might have verified by trapping what she'd seen, unfolding lifeless wings, then holding the creature next to a dog-eared field guide: "Yes, we were right: *Lasiurus cinereus*." We had had a word ready for a specimen. But now we realized that we had possessed no term for that larger, rapturous phenomenon we had been immersed in—despite how specifically and keenly we had tasted it with our skin and wanted to remain in its radiance. Finally we had its name: *bats!*

When it comes to experiencing the world with all one's senses, Emma has a big advantage over adults because—like other little children—she isn't a verbal thinker and is almost totally illiterate; her world is not conditioned by the linearity and distancing of an alphabet, grammatical "rules," and sentences. Another advantage is that, nearing age three, she has 50 percent more brain synapses than an adult. The metabolic activity in her brain exceeds adult levels and won't peak for another year, starting to decline only in her adolescence. What is she doing with so many sparks and switches crackling in her brain? Is she "thinking," and if so, how—especially without much language? By the time she's out of high school, her synapses will have decreased steadily in number until she's hobbling along like most grown-ups: every day less nimble mentally, more forgetful, more befogged. But at present, as a preschooler, she is capable of creating what appears to us adults to be spontaneous poetry, spinning elaborate narratives out of bits of plastic and a shoebox house, effortlessly naming and miming, absorbing and transforming phenomena.

But is it really thinking if it isn't articulate?

There are horse trainers in our neighborhood who are among the most laconic and nonverbal humans I've ever met. Yet they come as close as anyone I know to understanding how animals think and what they're thinking about. They seem to "hear" what hoofed animals are saying and "talk" to them in ways that indicate communication is going both ways. Most of these cowboys say that they learned horse-talk at the same time they learned human-talk, when they were children. Our farrier, Gabe, is an example. A couple of generations ago, he says, a lot more of his neighbors could do the kind of thinking he does. But today, many literate people—a group clearly in a powerful majority in society—seem to believe that the lack of verbal skills is a mark of low intelligence; some of the most highly literate even believe that there is no thought at all without language, that human beings are essentially "incarnated vocabularies."

Watching Gabe work on our donkey's hooves, I'm impressed by the way he seems to read the angle of an ear, the tensing of an ankle, a fluttering of the tail. I'm even more impressed that, in response, he makes himself understood by Magnolia's skittish donkey-soul.

I'm not about to say that Emma talks to donkeys—but it's possible that she may in some ways be thinking like them. When I watch Emma around animals, I see how she uses whole-body communication— although, to tell the truth, it appears that the animals are a lot more deft with what's going on than she is. Animals seem to know pretty much what Emma is thinking, and they seem to realize that, for now, she can't talk to them very well. And they are tolerant of her missteps. As she gets a little older, I suspect she'll have more agility with donkey-mind and goat-mind. But once she's beyond childhood, she'll have to practice frequently, in the physical presence of animals, or else she'll become as impoverished as most of her literate peers, who will know how to talk only to other humans.

Temple Grandin is an autistic woman who is a professor of animal sciences, having received her Ph.D. from the University of Illinois. Grandin has an uncanny ability to understand what animals are feeling and thinking. She says it's because she thinks in the same way animals do: not with language but through visual images. In her book *Thinking in Pictures and Other Reports from My Life with Autism*, Grandin explains: "Words are like a *second* language to me. I translate both spoken and written words into full-color movies, complete with sound, which run like a VCR tape in my head. When somebody speaks to me, his words are immediately translated into pictures." And she adds: "It is very likely that animals think in pictures and memories of smell, light,

and sound patterns. In fact, my visual thinking patterns probably re-
semble animal thinking more closely than those of verbal thinkers. . . .
Mine is a world of thinking that many language-based thinkers do not
comprehend. I have observed that the people who are most likely to
deny animals thought are often highly verbal themselves and have poor
visualization skills."

There are numerous examples of successful humans who are nonverbal thinkers. The list might include visual artists, musicians, and
dancers, as well as mathematicians, physicists, and engineers—people
who may be highly gifted at making and doing meaningful things,
but who can seem hobbled by speaking, writing, and reading. Einstein,
for example, didn't learn to talk until he was three years old; in his
autobiography he reported that, for him, "thoughts did not come in
any verbal formulation. I rarely think in words at all. A thought comes,
and I try to express it in words afterwards." Similarly, virologist Jonas
Salk explained, concerning his method of working: "I would picture
myself as a virus, or as a cancer cell, for example, and try to sense what
it would be like to be either. I would imagine myself as the immune
system."

Despite such examples of successful nonverbal thinkers, we might
easily get the impression from educational institutions and social hier-
archies that language mediates everything, and that all human experience, as the fashionable philosophers say, is "essentially linguistic." Animals and children demonstrate that this may be an exaggera-
tion, as anyone who has spent a lot of time with either can tell you.
Developmental psychologists and educators such as Merlin Donald
and Kieran Egan, building on the work of Lev Vygotsky and others, have written eloquently on childhood thinking. Though they
would not say that animal-mind and child-mind are the same, Vygotsky asserted that "the beginnings of practical intelligence in the
child . . . are independent of speech"; and Donald describes a prelin-
guistic thinking that involves understanding and communicating using
the whole body; he calls this "the most basic human thought skill . . .
independent of our linguistic modes of representation." Being with
animals affirms for children the nonlinguistic intelligence in our natures. As William James wrote, "Philosophy lives in words, but truth
and fact well up into our lives in ways that exceed verbal formulation.
There is in the living act of perception always something that glimmers
and twinkles and will not be caught, and for which reflection comes
too late."

According to his friend Gregory Bateson, Aldous Huxley contended that God is more like animals than like human beings, because God contains no internal confusions and cannot lie. Walt Whitman said something similar in his admiration of the simplicity and straight-forward nature of animals. Like many exceptional poets, Whitman respected what can't be said in words but is important nevertheless. "Writing and talk do not prove me," he wrote; "I carry the plenum of proof and everything else in my face, with the hush of my lips I confound the topmost skeptic." Rilke also felt that we get a glimpse of a purely nonlinguistic grace "when some animal, / mutely, serenely, looks us through and through." In Stephen Mitchell's translation of the "Eighth Elegy," Rilke says, "We know what is really out there only from / the animal's gaze; for we take the very young / child and force it around, so that it sees / objects—not the Open, which is so / deep in animals' faces." There is a stage of childhood, Rilke believed, that is so full of grace that its intelligence seems to arise from a Presence in the world that is continually gesturing to us, expecting us to understand what is being said and what response is called for.

In the Gospel of Matthew, the disciples ask Jesus, "Who is the greatest in the kingdom of heaven?" They may have been fishing to find out who among them was first in Christ's heart. But Jesus told them to bring a child to his side. "He put him in the midst of them," according to Matthew, "and said, 'Truly, I say unto you, unless you turn and become like children, you will never enter the kingdom of heaven.'"

Some have read this passage as Christ's (and Christianity's) desire to make the faithful passive. But that would be an inaccurate view of what children are—we might remember that when Jesus as a child confronted the rabbis in Jerusalem, he was anything but reticent and passive. Jesus' admonition to be like a child is very much like the Buddhist instruction to cultivate "beginner's mind," which means seeing the world as abundant and whole rather than as a prison house of Grammar and Things—to be utterly free, even of language. Shunryu Suzuki sums up this idea by asserting that you cannot find reality by vivisection.

When Lisa and I began to raise a clutch of ducklings last spring, we decided we had to exterminate the mongooses on our farm. Previously, we'd simply put up with these furtive creatures as they raided the goat barn for grain and burrowed through the compost. We'd catch a glimpse of them from the house in the late afternoons as they scurried

out of the tall grass of the pasture and up toward the garden. Because
mongooses avoid people and homes, it was easy for us to ignore them.
But the thought of the new ducklings being carried off and eaten by
mongooses made us reconsider.

Local mongooses are about a foot long and weigh about two
pounds. They have the face of a ferret, infernal red eyes, little X-Acto
teeth, and an aggressive temperament. The trap we used is made of galvanized steel. It's about four feet long and twelve inches square, with a
door at each end and a trigger in the middle that can be baited with a
raw egg. A nudge of the trigger makes the doors spring shut and lock.
Once we started trapping mongooses, we caught one every other day
for two weeks. To kill the ones we trapped, we'd throw the sprung de-
vice into the pond with the mongoose inside and let the whole thing
sink; then we'd drag the trap out by a rope tied to the handle. You could
almost hear underwater the hissing and the snapping of tiny teeth
against galvanized metal.

Exterminating a mongoose is something I'm reluctant to show
Emma, even though she sees most everything else that happens on our
farm. The little water-logged bodies we removed from the traps com-
pelled us to acknowledge our complicity in an act of horror. I know
that I haven't made my peace with killing varmints, and I haven't figured out how to talk to Emma about it, though eventually I know I
will. Animals live and die so completely in the present moment, their
essential natures seem to be saying something to us about eternity. It
can seem as if their gaze looks back across a frontier of silence into our
chattering world. Even the smallest of them place in front of us a silence in which nothing, not even death, can be disguised or avoided.
"Many things that human words have upset are set at rest again by
the silence of animals," Max Picard observed. "Animals move through
the world of words like a caravan of silence." With them, each moment's fullness already contains the erasure of their bodies, and so they
speak to our fear of losing this material existence. Their deaths make us
question what our lives will mean in a realm separate from human time,
in the eternity where animals already exist and where our deaths will
take us.

Moreover, when we acknowledge the actions that make us responsible for the deaths of animals—even inadvertent actions—our response reveals the condition of our souls. This revelation can be very
troubling, and will be the most difficult for me to explain to Emma. I
will have to talk about not only the suffering of a single mongoose, but

terrible, wasteful slaughter of domesticated animals. How will I talk to her about the holocaust of extinctions in wild habitats, or explain that the earth will be a substantially poorer place by the time she is grown up, with species now vanishing at the rate of one hundred per day worldwide?

Early in the last century, Rémy de Gourmont wrote, "There is no abyss between man and animal; the two domains are separated by a tiny rivulet which a baby could step over." I wonder at the difficulty that adults have in stepping over this rivulet, to join with animals in order to find a restorative empathy with the sentience all around us. I see Emma crossing that rivulet time and again. I suppose that, before I try to teach her about human cruelty and indifference, including my own, I want her to witness another part of herself—the potential of her heart to demonstrate, as Gourmont said, that "love is profoundly animal; therein is its beauty."

The hardest problem Emma has had to face on the farm up to now occurred last summer, when she grew fond of one of the baby goats. Each season we sell the male kids and keep only the females. Adult male goats smell very bad, especially during mating season. They get too big to handle, and they need separate pens built for them, away from the does. Overall, they aren't worth the trouble and extra expense they cause.

But when goats are babies, males are just as wonderful as females. Emma fell in love with one we named Homer, a black-and-white Nubian with floppy ears and springs in his legs. This was during the first summer that Emma was old enough to get into the paddocks with the goats, to see them as living things, different from herself and more willful. She waded through the toddler-high grass, laughing wildly as the kids bounded back and forth around her and cavorted in midair, their legs flying in all directions.

Homer and his twin sister were their young mother's first offspring, so we knew she might need help when her time came. Unfortunately, a premature delivery caught us off guard. We weren't there for the mother until the next morning. Being inexperienced, she rejected the two undersized lumps whimpering at her feet and wouldn't let them nurse. She just stared and murmured in confusion.

Initially, both kids had to be bottle-fed day and night, and then less frequently for several weeks. Emma helped by holding the bottle for Homer, who eagerly dropped to his knees in front of her and vigorously wagged his tale, sucking noisily and prodding at the rubber nipple. Emma held on tightly to the bottle and squealed with giddy surprise. The milk ran down Homer's chin and dried to a thick, sweet crust.

Day by day, with constant attention, Homer grew stronger. He recognized Emma whenever she entered the paddock, and the two of them played together. After about twelve weeks, it came time to sell Homer. Lisa found a buyer, and she and Emma put the young goat into the cab of the truck and drove him forty miles down the coast into Hilo. On the way, Lisa explained what was about to happen.

Days later, Emma was still asking occasionally where Homer had gone. "To live on another farm," Lisa repeated, "where he has lots of new goat friends and a bigger paddock."

"Doesn't he miss his mother and sisters?"

"Probably a little. But goats aren't like people. They grow up fast, and Homer is very happy where he is," I explained.

Emma let that news cook for a while. Then she named a toy sheep after Homer and regularly quizzed him to be sure he was okay in a new home so far away from us. She gave this surrogate Homer some medicine for his diarrhea, checked him for lice, fed him with a toy bottle, and tucked him into bed. In this way, Homer entered Emma's mythological world, where his name continues to evoke—for Lisa and me, as well as Emma—a cosmos of feelings and thoughts too abundant and subtle for ordinary language to describe.

JOHN BOWER

Slowing Down
Robins, Owen, and Evolution

Nine A.M. and I am introducing a group of sleepy college students to a Pacific Northwest old-growth forest. Some stand silent and awestruck, staring up at the massive crowns of the two-hundred-foot-tall Douglas firs. Others laugh and giggle as they make human rings around the tree trunks. One student discovers what she thinks is a fallen tree, but as we look at it, I realize it is actually a huge Douglas fir root, so big around that it is a challenge to climb over. After about twenty minutes of such delights I encourage them to pay attention to the subtler stories of the forest—epiphytes and lichens growing on big-leafed maples, saprophytic flowering plants stealing nutrients from other plants' roots. A few students end up on their hands and knees, captured by the forest's mysteries, but for most the thrill is gone. Yawns start to appear—they are done with this forest. A half hour visiting a six-hundred-year-old forest and they are ready to move on.

Moving on—it is the modern way. After three years on the job, I know the challenges: digging beneath the rubble left by memorize-and-regurgitate high school science courses, helping students shed their American late-adolescent, high-stimulus culture for long enough to see nature's subtler excitement, and simply slowing them down in the hopes that a chance meeting with a plant or animal will draw them closer to the natural world.

Later, after this field trip's typical moderate success and an unhealthy dose of my own breakneck university pace, I am home—tired, but ready to start the parenting portion of my day. My partner is exhausted from eight hours with the kids, so both are mine to entertain for awhile. Maggie, my three-month-old daughter, is running at my speed—she needs a nap. Babies have odd requirements—at this age, she will consent to going to sleep in my arms only if I am outdoors. Owen is another story. Full of three-year-old energy, excited at my arrival, his need for high-energy play is far beyond what I can currently muster. My most recent solution to this situation is a new lawn sprinkler. I set the sprinkler to throw its arc back and forth across the back of our small urban backyard, and perch on the picnic bench with Maggie stretched out along my forearm, staring at the grass and gnawing on my skin while she settles. Owen responds immediately, peeling off his clothes and sprinting across the yard just ahead of or behind the water—screaming in delight when he manages to outsmart the sprinkler and screaming just as loudly when caught by its cold spray.

All is stable for the moment. My thoughts return to my morning field trip. I contemplate the modern pace. Even if I order my students to walk slowly, stay near me, try their hand at identifying a few plants, fewer than half of them will manage it for more than a couple of hundred feet. They simply can't maintain that slow a pace. I tell them about John Muir propping himself up against a giant sequoia for an entire day and they groan—they need to be walking, running, and talking; their pace is calibrated to video games, cell phones, and MTV. I lecture them: "To know nature requires moving slowly. You all tell me how much you want to heal the earth. You'll never know enough about nature to do it without first slowing down and letting nature set the pace." A few take the challenge; most roll their eyes.

What some of them must be thinking, though no one ever says, is that I am a complete hypocrite—my pace is even faster than theirs, set by the university madness: teaching, writing, committee work, and by my commitment to be fully involved in a rich family life. Students must be aware of this since they are well aware of the tricks required to talk to me alone—ambushes in the hall, sneaking into my lab on a Saturday. I was hired at least partly to study nature, and in particular bird behavior, but when do I have time anymore to slow down enough to hear nature speaking, to share a bird's life for more than a passing moment? In graduate school I spent three springs in the same old farm field, day after day, deeply immersed in the issues of a dozen song sparrow families. I shared their triumphs and tragedies, the big moments of their lives. Two males brutally fighting for a territory in a cold March rain, their fight interrupted by a Cooper's hawk drawn to their raucous encounter with mortal intent. A male's excited dance with fanned tail and drooping wings as last year's female partner approaches him for the first time after seven months apart. The hatching of babies and the intense work required to get them out of the nest in twelve days and self-sufficient in another twelve. The morning after a raccoon attack, the grasses from the nest strewn about while one dying nestling lies panting on the ground. The adults flit around chirping for an hour or two before turning their attention to building a new nest for a new chance to bring forth life. It is a level of seeing and knowing nature that few people achieve today—far beyond the occasional walk in the woods. I believe it has special lessons, lessons I desperately want to share with my children. But seeing those things requires moving far more slowly than this culture dictates. Even if I can achieve it, will my children be willing?

In my current life, the nature I know results from serendipity—quick observations made through the kitchen window while washing dishes, flashes of natural moments observed while making unplanned nursing stops along the drive to Seattle. I try to keep up with the local residents: a white-crowned sparrow, who, even after nearly three months of regularly singing his buzzy short song has not managed to attract a mate to our neighborhood. A weeklong songbird feeding frenzy (forty-three yellow-rumped warblers and six orange-glowing male western tanagers at the same time!) in the insect-infested silver maple next to our driveway. A fly-by bird-feeder attack by a sharp-shinned hawk. Nature has become the subtext of my life, occasional cameos in a high-speed modern script.

A female robin alighting on the wood fence brings me back from my thoughts. She stands silently surveying the scene for about twenty seconds, flicking her tail nervously—apparently intent on flying down to the grass despite Owen's running and screaming. Suddenly, she drops down into the far corner of the yard and starts foraging in the grass. Another lucky nature vignette. Maggie in my arms, the bird tolerating Owen—I hope to join this robin's world for a few seconds.

I'm surprised to see her—robins have not been conspicuous for several weeks. I've seen a few flying and have heard some singing at dawn and calling at dusk, but otherwise they have disappeared from the conspicuous bird scene. A mystery—what have they been up to and why this sudden appearance? I think about late June in a robin's world. The first brood is probably raised by now, the young fledged and off in juvenile flocks in some nearby forested park. What is she up to now?

She is hunting very actively—and successfully. After less than a minute she pulls a worm from the soil. Instead of eating it, she swings her bill around in the air rhythmically, looping the worm several times over her lower mandible. I realize I've never seen this looping behavior before. By now Owen has stopped running, having also noticed her. I delight in the observational powers of small children and, selfishly, in my child's interest in birds and beckon him to share the robin minute with me. He runs over to me, takes a vacant knee, and immediately starts asking questions: "Is it a mommy or daddy robin?" I explain the difference in head color—gray in mommies, black in daddies. This is a mommy. "Where are the baby robins?" I don't know if she has any babies; how do you think we could tell? Owen is a child, I am a biologist—I am asking questions too. "Why would she insist on visiting our high-use backyard?" I wonder out loud. Now Owen has the answer, "Because she likes us, Daddy." Just then the robin runs directly under the sprinkler and tugs a second long earthworm from the soil. Owen squeals in excitement—predation and death have been high on his animal behavior wish list lately. She loops this one around her bill as she did the first, and flies in a direct line to a cottonwood half a block away. Owen knows just where she is going—to feed her babies. She must be feeding a new brood. The robin's recent low profile was probably due to incubating the second brood—a good time to avoid notice.

A minute later, she is back. "Must be great worm hunting here," I say, and with a flash, another mystery is solved: Recent water conservation efforts have convinced most people in our neighborhood to let their yards go brown during the Northwest's summer dry season. Given my own historically excellent water conservation record, I decided I deserve to indulge my child in summer sprinkler pleasures, particularly since the partial closure of our local paper mill has made millions of gallons of extra water available this summer. Owen's initial excitement about sprinkler games has greened the lawn considerably in one week. With the daily watering, worms must be staying close to the surface to avoid drowning. Owen's water games are no doubt contributing to the enhanced survival of the robin's offspring. Owen and I work through the logic of this explanation while Maggie continues to gnaw on my forearm.

One mystery solved; others are born. I share them with Owen: "How often does she visit?" "How long after the water stops does our yard remain a fertile hunting ground?" He chimes in: "Where is the daddy bird?" I stop. Great question—where is the daddy? "I don't know where the daddy is." Owen goes back to play, but returns to continue our observations every time the robin shows up. She returns several more times without a break, always hunting, tugging, and looping two or three worms before returning to the same maple tree. In the twenty minutes we have been watching her, she has been hunting, flying, or feeding the entire time. The male has been missing in action. I know that robin males share the caring for young, and with such an excellent food source present I'm surprised the male is not hunting here as well.

Then he arrives. He sits on the fence for longer than the female did. Owen is excited that the daddy robin has arrived. In Owen's world, no story is complete without a mommy, a daddy, and babies. Finally, the male glides down to the lawn and begins to stalk earthworms. He hunts more slowly and less intensely than the female. After about two minutes he finally pulls a worm from the grass. And then eats it. I point this out to Owen, and he is visibly disturbed. "Why didn't he take the worm to his babies?" I have a hunch, but for now I keep it to myself. Darwin's theory of sexual selection provides a potent hypothesis: In most bird species females have greater investment in their young since they produce the energetically expensive eggs. And, they work correspondingly harder to raise them. Even in socially monogamous birds, the mother typically works harder than the father in feeding the young.

While he is searching for his second worm, the female arrives again. There is a short interaction between them—a little chase—and then she goes right back to work. I wonder if he will change his habits with her present. He doesn't hunt any faster, but he does fly off to the same cottonwood with the next worm he catches. Over the next half hour, this pattern repeats itself: When the female is present, the male takes worms back to the nest; when she is absent, he eats them. All the while the female is working steadily, and I never see her eat a worm. The possibility of deceit crosses my mind: does he eat the worms when she is absent to increase his ability to survive—in essence, taking advantage of her highly charged feeding effort?

While Owen is off on another sprinkler run, I consider whether to make these ideas known to him. I delight in sharing my observations, and I am thrilled that, so far anyway, my son is a willing and even enthusiastic partner in my occasional nature observations. But evolutionary biologists don't just observe; we interpret our observations within an evolutionary framework—creating and testing new hypotheses to discover how evolution has shaped nature. When I am in nature, my mind is rarely silent—it tells stories and asks questions about what I am seeing. I think of the surprise I felt when I realized that Owen was honing this skill. He had accompanied me on a class camping trip to the San Juan Islands and, after dinner, fed up with my focusing on students all day, he whispered in my ear that he wanted to take a walk with me to see some deer. So, we bushwhacked out from our campsite for an evening deer stalk. As we made our way through the thick brush, we stumbled across three trees lying together on the forest floor. A large Douglas fir and a smaller western hemlock were dead, but a second hemlock was lying on the ground, throwing up new growth from its skyward branches. It looked as though a dozen hemlocks were growing out of the living hemlock's trunk. As we examined it, Owen, who had been along on an earlier class walk, suddenly adopted a quasi-professorial voice and explained to me how the whole scenario had come to be. The dead fir fell, knocking over the hemlocks that had been growing out of its trunk. With sadness in his voice he told of how both hemlocks wanted to survive, but that one had died, and then with glee he explained how the other hemlock was growing up into the sky in a new way. His tale of death and survival had all the elements of a coherent evolutionary story.

Owen's natural tale delighted me in the same way that a person in business must feel when a child discovers how the stock market works. But it also troubled me: while evolution is a powerful tool for explaining nature, it can also be a troubling knowledge, one that runs in the face of how humans have interpreted nature for thousands of years. For my students, nature is largely a beautiful inspiration, providing peaceful meditative moments and inspiration for living. Many believe in the literal truth of the Gaia hypothesis—animals and plants primarily act to take care of each other and the earth. Nature, they argue, should be a model for human behavior. I understand the appeal of this belief: if only we can rid ourselves of our artificial human-created characteristics and get back to nature, we will find long-lasting love and happiness and heal the environment at the same time. Nothing really new in that thought—turn-of-the-century ministers commonly used the example of how a pair of songbirds work hard to raise their young to implore humans (and particularly men) to dedicate themselves to monogamy and to their families.

But the evolutionary view of nature sees competition as a stronger shaping force than cooperation. Darwin's theories were based on competition between species and competition between individuals in a species. More recently, it has become clear that the apparent cooperation we witness between a pair of birds is an uneasy partnership, made all the more difficult, recent discoveries show, by the fact that songbird nests often include several young fathered by neighbors. There is clearly much room for conflict between the robins hunting in our yard as each attempts to maximize its own reproduction.

Being a biologist, I've always thought I'd be ahead of the game, as

I have few problems talking about such natural phenomena as sex or death. But as I sit and watch a male robin taking it easy while the female works nonstop, and even see some evidence that he may be deceiving her, I feel myself suppressing the urge to share this with my son. What would I tell him—that mommies often work harder than daddies at taking care of the children? Moving into the realm of deception and conflict between daddies and mommies seems wrought with perils. Would Owen start to worry about these possibilities within his own family? Would I be nudging him along toward a solely materialistic view of the world? And the bigger question: as I gradually disseminate my evolutionary worldview to my son, am I committing the same category of sin I accuse many parents of doing through church-school indoctrination?

For the moment, like a 1960s parent creating private illusions to avoid discussing sex, I evade the issue. I tell myself that I will share this type of knowledge later in life, though as I sift through the coming years in my mind, I gain no clear sense of the appropriate age for revealing these ideas. Maggie is asleep and ready to be put down. It is nearing six o'clock, and neither my partner nor I have started dinner preparations. There is a bath to be had, books to be read, a bedtime video, and I still have two hours' worth of student papers to read. The never-ending list of what needs to be done becomes my excuse. I call Owen away from the sprinkler, away from the robins, and into the house. The robins and the questions they inspire slip back into the slower world—for now.

DAVID SOBEL

Assessing Ice
A Father and Daughter's Coming of Age

Ode to Winter

There's a Wallace Stevens poem called "The Snow Man" that's been snagged in my mind for the last thirty years, about as long as I've been heading to the Caribbean for a couple of weeks right after Christmas each year. As the solstice approaches, I recite the first line, "One must have a mind of winter / To regard the frost and the boughs / Of the pine-trees crusted with snow," and I welcome the sparse truth of leaflessness, the relaxing of preparation. Heading south has increasingly felt like a bioregional betrayal to me, a slap in the face of winter mind, a seasonal sin. Just as the quiet settles like a heavy quilt and the lakes drift off to sleep, I hearken to the beat of the steel drum and toss down piña coladas. "It just isn't natural," whispers the little angel on my right shoulder. "Have you forgotten your pledge of allegiance to the snow queen?"

And so I feel a bit embarrassed as I jet off to Tobago, Vieques, or Provodenciales to snorkle, surf, and snarf. Dine on mango salsa and grilled kingfish. Descend jungle trails to coral coves of sugar sand and plunge into the rebellious mambo #5 waves that have never learned good manners, have never had to sit quietly in one place and be seen and not heard.

Two winters ago, the winter of 1998–99, the freeze came hard and fast in mid-December. After weeks of relative warmth, it plunked down to below zero for three nights in a row with no wind. "Yes, Master!" the waters bowed obsequiously and prostrated themselves. Black ice slithered across the shallower ponds. I ignore the road and glance through the trees down to Robb Reservoir as I drive to work, and a hunger rises in me when this first pure ice appears. I leave work a bit early on Friday and use the lingering twilight to check the ice on Child's Bog. Three or four inches of spooky transparency. Daunting to the nerves but satin to the skate blades.

On Saturday, my daughter Tara and her friend Erin join me in the first exploration. We are tentative in the beginning. Down on hands and knees to check the depths of the cracks, cautious around stumps and boulders, hesitant as we move further away from shore, flinching at the rolling thunder of ice expansion. But as it becomes apparent that it is unquestionably solid everywhere, we become giddy and playful. We circumnavigate the long cove-y shoreline, weaving in and out of fallen trees that stick out of the ice. We lie facedown and peer into the inky depths, and lick the ice hoping our tongues won't stick. We tow each other by our skates, race between outcrops, try to make the perfect set of lilting blade marks. Finding the absolute middle of the pond, we lie on our backs and take in the full saucer of spruce-rimmed sky.

When we return from our Caribbean idyll, the ice is gone, buried under soggy snow, never to reappear again that winter. We pay homage to winter in our downhill skiing adventures, but there's a piece of me that misses ice, misses the playful exploration with Tara. As the following December unfolds, cold, still, and snowless, the opportunity for absolution unfolds.

Father and Daughter

There's another story here as well, the story about my relationship with my daughter, who is thirteen at the millennium. Much of my parenting energy has been dedicated to being a good dad—being emotionally present, telling family stories, supporting my children's individuality, teaching social responsibility, structuring appropriate challenges, and forging an immutable bond with the natural world. I have always believed that there is a window of opportunity in middle childhood for developing a love of nature, for experiencing that deep interpenetration between self and wildness. At the same time, I am a strong believer in developing physical competence in childhood as the foundation for a firm sense of self. Childhood should be a time for children to discover their bodies through bicycling, climbing trees, jumping rope, playing hopscotch, skateboarding, and all manner of developing kinesthetic coordination.

It's odd, those idiosyncratic bits of conversations, like shards of poetry, that get lodged in memory. They reveal potency and personal meaning. They intimate directions. Such was a fleeting comment from a graduate student after a conversation about parenting in my Human Development course more than ten years ago. "I am really indebted to my parents for their commitment to teaching me to ski," Nancy Segreto reflected. "Starting at about six or seven and all the way through my adolescence, we trucked off to Vermont most weekends in the winter. Learning to ski gave me a deep sense of centeredness, an irrefutable balance and self-confidence, a calmness in the face of risk, that I have carried into all other aspects of my life." At that moment, a seed of resolve was planted. I had never been much of a skier, hadn't tried skiing until high school, and had always been a bit of a klutz. Though competent as a cross-country skier, I had always longed for that inner sense of balance, the confidence to plummet down steep slopes with refined abandon. And it jibed nicely with my mind of winter. "We will be a skiing family," I decided at that moment. I wanted my children to have that internal assuredness.

But skiing was just the speck of dust at the center of the snowflake. I like encouraging my children to rub up against the cold edges of the world. They have become polar bears with me, taking up the challenges of cold-water swimming. They've learned the inexorable beauty of black ice. They have a taste for white water, dark woods, double-diamond slopes, and high jumps into deep water. Each spring we head off for the day to Bear Dens State Park to search for new boulder caves. They've left me behind in their willingness to squirm into grotey places. I beamed with quiet pride last spring as Eli, age eleven, agreed to go down a tunnel about three feet in diameter along a tongue of still-melting, pebble-encrusted ice. Tara, now thirteen, willingly followed him into the inky blackness. "Awesome!" her voice echoed up. "It's a big room, there's a porcupine den at the back, and it's like a big refrigerator because there's still a lot of ice down here."

Encounters with ice, or the essence of ice, or iciness, that's one of the threads here. And encountering adolescence, that's the other thread. Have you seen the 1997 film *Fly Away Home* — the rite-of-passage film about a girl's relationship with a flock of Canada geese? To help her save the geese, her father teaches her to fly an ultralite airplane. In separate planes they head south from Ontario to North Carolina to resettle the geese in a winter home. It's about ecological restoration, closeness to beauty, rising to the challenge, and the father's letting go of his daughter. I didn't just tear up at the ending; I cried all the way through it and pretty much sobbed at the ending, despite the corniness. Sobbed because I understood it expressed what I had been trying to do and what I had to do.

The persistent developmental question for me over the past few years, as Tara has moved toward and through puberty, has been this: does adolescence have to be a time of turmoil and angry separation from parents? I'll be talking with other parents about enjoying cooking dinner with Tara, or about a charming Thanksgiving morning walk we enjoyed. "How old is Tara now?" they'll ask. When I reply that she's thirteen, they'll respond, "Oh you're just getting to the hard part, the things-fall-apart years. Just you wait!" I nod in acquiescence, acknowledging the cultural myth, but inwardly I resist. I am not sure that things have to fall apart.

Margaret Mead, in her study of adolescent girls in Samoa in the 1920s, framed an analogous question: "Are the disturbances which vex our adolescents due to the nature of adolescence itself or to the civilization? Under different conditions does adolescence present a different picture?" And more specifically, for adolescent girls, she questioned, "Can we think of adolescence as a time in the life history of every girl child which carries with it symptoms of conflict and stress as surely as it implies a change in the girl's body?" Based on her observation of Samoan girls, her conviction was that there were not great differences between girls before and after puberty. She felt it was American culture that created adolescent angst. Similarly, my sense has been that the turmoil and anger of adolescence are in small part hormonal and biological, and in large part a cultural artifact. In many ways, as parents and as a society, we create the problems of adolescence and, conversely, we can create the different conditions that Margaret Mead refers to. Perhaps if we did it right in schools, in our families, and in our communities, we could avoid many of these problems.

Carol Gilligan and other feminist developmental theorists have pointed to the ways in which girls flourish in late childhood. They are sturdy, self-assured, confident. And then at twelve or thirteen they go underground, lose their forthrightness. I didn't want that to happen with Tara. And much of how I've parented has been in anticipation of this issue. One of my intended solutions has been to forge a relationship built on shared adventure in the natural world. If I could give her that sense of inner strength that comes from wisely choosing personal challenges and meeting them, perhaps she'd stay on top of the ground rather than going underground. If we practiced meeting challenges together, then perhaps I could gently let her go off to take risks on her own at the appropriate time. And perhaps the tangible metaphors of taking the plunge, setting your edges, and getting back on the horse could provide instructive guidance for the abstract dilemmas ahead.

"More confirmation of global warming," we all grumbled as November 1999 stretched on warm and dry. But then winter snapped its fingers in mid-December, a quick, hard freeze without a hint of snow. I waited in anticipation, looking for frozen coves, evaluating the shape and size of the patches of open water. Each morning I'd poke a stick through the skim of ice on the frog pond, only a half inch, barely more than an inch. When it warmed up to the thirties and forties, I regretted the setback. But then a few days before the solstice, below zero. Some people wait for four inches of ice. I'm comfortable with three, and will consider two when the body of water is small and shallow. I talked Eli into the inaugural skate. By nine o'clock, the fullest moon of the century, high in the solstice night sky, was floodlighting the pond. Avoiding the end down by the big rock where a spring keeps the ice mushy in the beginning of the season, we swooped and scraped, finding our skating legs after almost a year. Cold butts sitting on the ice, we speculated that we might be the only people skating that night, because none of the larger bodies of water were solid enough. It was too cold for more than a short skate, but it whetted my appetite. This year, for the first year in almost twenty years, we weren't going south. Perhaps this year, we could really skate.

On Christmas we have a rowdy game of hockey with three families of moms and dads and boys and girls ages eight to fourteen at a friend's house in Peterborough. Lots of bumps and bruises, but mostly the excitement of friendly competitiveness, of parents and children embraced in good-natured tussling. The edginess of fast hockey, of imagining elbows impacting ice, of cold-bitten toes and frosted noses, made us glow with exhilaration. Pond hockey feels like part of the birthright of being a northern New Englander (read that as north of the Mason-Dixon line of the Massachusetts border). You have to know and trust ice, and abandon yourself to intuitive skating, to succeed at hockey. It's rough, ragged, and exhausting—the crucible of true grit. I love seeing Tara mix it up and steal the puck from one of the dads and whip around to take a shot on goal.

December 30, 1999. After a couple of shorter outings, the next to the last day of the millennium dawns still and warm. "Highs in the upper twenties," is music to our ears; twenty-nine degrees is the grail temperature for exploratory skaters. Cold enough to keep the ice intact, warm enough to feel cozy once the blood gets pumping. Tara willingly takes up my invitation to foray back up the stream that feeds into Harrisville Pond, a long, slightly risky skate this early in the winter. The moving water of the marshy stream, especially over the frequent beaver dams, will make for thin ice and constant vigilance.

We park at the beach near the center of the village—an old haunt. Tara has grown up here, learning to swim, collecting garnets at the water's edge, picking blueberries, experimenting with distance swimming. We lace up at the picnic table, clomp across the sand, and pick our way over the refrozen, wave-driven slush for the first couple hundred yards. But then, it's as if the courtiers have rolled out the velvet carpet for the queen; the black ice is immaculate. Beyond the point where she and Cary swam out to last summer, the horizon of personal exploration, the familiar starts to fade.

As we approach the mouth of the stream, I explain the challenges ahead. We discuss the strategies of assessing ice, of regularly checking cracks to determine depth, of looking for the changes in the surface texture that suggest water movement underneath. We discuss the wisdom of carrying a long branch to catch on the ice in case of a breakthrough and to use to push off the bottom to get back on the ice. We make plans for what to do if you're trying to help someone who has broken through—remain calm, spread out your weight as much as possible, don't get too close to the edge of broken ice as you're trying to rescue someone to make sure you don't go in as well. In part, I am training her in close observation of the subtleties of the landscape. It is a seminar in risk assessment: knowing that it's fun to push the limits and sneak back into inaccessible places, but also knowing the limits to pushing the limits, knowing when to say no, this isn't safe anymore.

Tara remembers it this way.

As an end to this century and a beginning of the next, Daddy and I have decided to go on as many skating expeditions as we can before the ice turns bad. Today was a good one to start them off. We went to Harrisville Pond, a place I thought I knew, but I found it unseemingly mysterious. We laced up our skates and glided back to where a small stream flows in. Avoiding thin ice and small sections of open water, we made our way back through brush and reeds and sometimes over land. It was quite scary, though the day was bright and clear, looking down and seeing through the ice to where the rushes on the bottom swayed in the current. By moving steadily, lying spread-eagle when we crossed, constantly checking the depth of the ice, and skating extremely slowly and cautiously, we made it successfully back to where the stream got too thin

to keep going. Here we lay down on the ice, faces toward the sun, and recol-
lected good times of the past century that we had shared together. We then
skated back with a sense of freedom, not having to pay attention to every cross-
ing point in the stream. A happy way to end a happy year.

We dawdle on the way back. The stillness of the afternoon reminds me of slack tide, those few moments after the tide has stopped coming in and hasn't yet started going out. The breeze drops, ceaselessness ceases, time naps. At a rope swing we make ourselves into drawing compasses, inscribing geometrical circles in the ice. We skate by Jack's place and Tara points out the fallen tree on the edge of the pond where she and Linnea hid during a twilight Sardines game last Fourth of July. We had searched and searched and never been able to find them.

I feel a sense of anticipatory nostalgia. The afternoon glistens with such perfection that I already feel the missing. I want it to stay this way forever, this moment of beauty, this closeness with Tara, but the tide turns. All the talk of assessing ice and measuring risk has a subtext. Tara's body is filling out, boyfriends are starting to enter the scene, she feels the urge for adventure and separation. I am preparing her metaphorically for the dark night on a city street when she needs to be guarded, attentive to cues in the landscape. Is it safe to proceed? I want her to be able to assess the risks of getting into a car driven by some guy she doesn't know after a party. We are rehearsing her departure.

Looking Back: Setting an Edge

True to my original commitment, I started Tara skiing at six. Though Tara was outdoorsy, she never had much of a sense of balance. Learning to ride a bike was difficult and traumatic for her, and much as I tried to be patient, some of my worst parenting moments occurred during bike lessons. One session that started with my sincerest resolve to stay calm ended with my muttering "F— the bike!" as I tossed it into the woods. I hoped skiing would be different, for both her and me.

It was. We spent a number of afternoons on the rope tow at Temple Mountain, often with her on a strap out in front of me, sometimes with her holding on to the handle of my outstretched ski pole. We did the same boring slope over and over until things fell into place.

Over the last six or seven years, Eli, Tara, and I have become mildly serious skiers. I have lots of questions about industrial skiing, and the ecological impacts of snowmaking, stream reductions, massive sewage treatment, and habitat fragmentation. But for me and my kids, it's been worth it. We love the camaraderie of early departures, weird conditions, and virgin corduroy. Throughout the summer we talk fondly of memorable slopes — of the fresh powder on Mythmaker that day at Attitash, of the impossible death cookies on that ungroomed slope at Killington, the great side trails on Chipmunk at Sunapee.

This past winter, Tara and I fell into our own private moguls seminar. At the beginning of the winter we were both at the same place, wanting to be able to ski bumps, but always feeling defeated once we were in them. At the dentist's office, I always flip to the "Seven Ways to Get the Bumps under Control" article in *Ski* magazine, study the pictures, try to follow the abstruse directions, and sigh. "I really want to get bumps!" Tara exclaimed with frustration after an unsuccessful run early in the winter.

We got our first chance on a windy, gray day at Haystack in southern Vermont. A couple of times a winter, I take one kid out of school on Tuesdays for an illicit ski day. Tuesday is the unbusiest day of the week, and the emptiness heightens the experience of confronting your fears. You're out here alone.

After a quick warm-up run we head for the Witches, a set of four black diamond runs that get increasingly difficult as you move from north to south. Today, we thought, we will get bumps. Since it had snowed six inches on Monday, we figured we were in for a day of freshly groomed powder. But as we rode up the lift, the wind started to howl, and as we slipped down Wizard, the easiest of the four, we found a patchwork of ungroomed heavy snow and ice-glazed moguls, a difficult combination. I was willing to abandon the attempt, scared of hurting myself, but Tara wanted to press on. "Here's an opportunity to let her take the lead," I thought to myself. Another run on Wizard and Tara reflected, "You've got to be prepared for the change in speed between the ice and the thick snow, and you've got to get going fast enough to get your skies to maneuver in the heavy stuff." Observation and assessment. As we rode the lift over Gandalf, the hardest slope, we watched competent skiers. "Look at the way he's hopping, lots of short turns with a quick edge set," she pointed as we peered down from the chair, trying to feel the quick momentum changes in our bodies. I liked the way we were equal partners in this process. I didn't have a corner on the skill market; we were both trying to figure it out together, in a collegial rather than a parent/child fashion.

After a somewhat successful run on more-challenging Cauldron, we talked each other into taking the plunge on Gandalf. And though I basically fell apart on the hard part, Tara was waiting with a big smile on her face at the bottom. "I actually got it! I could feel it in my body for the first time!" she enthused. I felt envious.

Class meeting number two. A cut-glass day, cold and sparkly. We head over to The Outpost lift at Pico, an old double that's tucked away in a corner, always neglected. Another set of short, ungroomed, moguly black diamonds. We ski the first couple and I feel a hint of competence, but Tara is seriously in the groove, getting just the right punctuated rhythm. Nora, a friend of hers, joins us and wants to ski Sidewinder, a twisty little trail off by itself, by far the hardest of the set. She's leaning on Tara to try it, and Tara is looking sheepish, hesitant, and scared. The entrance is barely wider than a hallway, and right away it drops out of sight around a sharp turn. I can tell from the lay of the land that it has to descend over a little bit of a cliff in the upper third somewhere. It will tax Tara's skill level. But I don't tell her that. I know it's beyond me, but I suspect it's within what Vygotsky calls her "zone of proximal development." In other words, it will be achievably challenging, but not overwhelming, I hope. I'm nervous for her, but I don't show it, and I gently nudge her to try it. My job is to stand back and let her take the challenge by herself. When she gets to the bottom, she's wide-eyed, breathless, and exhilarated.

Later that day, we talk each other into a trail we've looked at for a couple of years, and have always avoided. It's one of those off-the-summit, under-the-lift trails, a whale of a trail. With not really enough snow on it, it's ledgy and scraped off, lots of brush obstacles. But we're both feeling a little bit cocky, so we take a deep breath and drop down over the cornice. Usually, skiing under lifts makes us feel like bugs under a magnifying glass. We both dislike being watched. Today, however, nobody else is skiing this trail, and we look like the hotshots that we usually gawk at. As we competently pick our way down, avoiding gravel, carving quick, linked turns, we're both tickled with ourselves. We aced that quiz.

The final exam happens about a month later at Sugarbush. Many of the lifts are on windhold, but one summit lift is operating. We're intimidated as the chairs start to sway in the gale, but both Tara and Eli are game when I suggest we ski Ripcord, the double diamond straight down the face. My journal excerpt from that evening recounts:

Mashed potatoes and boilerplate. Sheets of windblown snow, ragged bumps, yelling above the gale. Eli schussing down with few problems, Tara a bit more cautious but holding her own. I watch as she loses a ski under the lift, way above me. Nothing to do but wait. She clambers up the hill, tries to find a flat spot to snap back in, the wind almost blowing her over. A long, awkward struggle, but soon she's back in the groove. I motion Eli to keep going and we descend separately. Eli below, Tara above, spindrift assaulting the corner of my goggles, I feel a fatherly pride. Yes! Double diamond family freedom. Cold grit, silver-tinted fear, quiet composure. My kids and I in the grip, alone and together, my confidence in their muscles and bones. Tara, once shaky and tethered to me, now making precise, clean-edged turns on the hard crust. Later on she said, "I wasn't scared, I just knew I needed to take it really slow. I knew I'd make it down, just not very gracefully."

The proof of the pudding came one evening after dinner about a week later. I was washing dishes and Tara was putting the food away. She'd just started taking snowboard lessons in her school ski program. A great opportunity to hang with friends and try a new challenge. With no prompting from me, she offered, "You know, about three weeks ago, I'd taken my first boarding lesson and I was heading up to the lodge and Rose, Anna, and Cary called to me to ride the lift up with them. I'd only been on the bunny slope and my first thought was that I was scared to go up the lift—the slope would be too hard. But then I thought, 'Hey, I can do this, I don't need to be afraid.' And so I went up with them and I could really do it. I'm so happy you taught me how to ski, Daddy, because it's really given me self-confidence. I can get past being afraid now because I know how to face risks calmly and not get overwhelmed." No kidding. She really said that. I was pleased as punch.

In Our Wild Backyard

January 2, 2000. It's been raining for a couple of days, and water is ponding on the ice. I'm concerned our ice forays are stymied, but I'm not willing to give up that easily. Mindful of that old Outward Bound saying that "there is no such thing as bad weather, just inappropriate clothing," I want to model persistence, and stick-to-it-ness. I'm also trying to treat staying at home for the holidays like being on vacation. When we go away, there's always familial energy for going on adventures, searching out new corners of the landscape. At home, it's easy to fall into the habitual outings—the walk to the gorge, or down to the Lion's Club field, the same old–same old. With no school and no work, we've got the opportunity to be bold and strike out for new terrain. Even though I've lived in the Monadnock region for more than twenty-five years, it doesn't take much to push beyond the familiar. And if we were on vacation, we wouldn't let a little drizzle slow us down. Our neighbor Erin joined us. Tara recalls:

Today was quite a dreary day, but we decided we must go out for another adventure, because we hadn't been out for a whole two days. (Gasp!) We were slightly afraid that the rain had ruined the ice, and we prayed it would not start up again. Our first try, Chesham Pond, was horrible—in some places up to four inches of water on the ice. Our second destination, a little pond in Roxbury we'd never been to, was a little better, and the ice wasn't as mushy, so we concluded that small ponds might be better. I was ready to go home because it was getting late, but Daddy wanted to try Clapp Pond, another new one. I was getting bored with lacing, unlacing, and relacing my skates.

We followed a little trail down through the woods to a dark, narrow pond. By the time we had our skates on, it was almost four o'clock, the light was dim, and the mist and fog were getting denser as the night set in. Too eerie for skating! Though covered with water in lots of places, the ice was actually OK. After some time of what felt like floating two or three inches above the pond, we made it down to the beaver pond in the outlet where we found the lodge and food sticks stored by the beaver. We had to carefully tiptoe around on the thin ice. Erin and I felt shivers when we heard the ice crack, but no one fell in.

On the way up the pond on the other side, we discovered an old tree tipped over with its root system sticking up out of the ice, maybe ten feet tall. All the dirt and earth that you usually see hanging from those things was gone, so it made an interweaving mazelike sculpture of old roots. Two of us would go behind it and stick our heads in the openings. Then the third person would get you to tilt your head sideways, or position it anyway they pleased to make a strange, beheaded masterpiece. By that time it was almost dark and our feet were really wet and cold, so we headed back, periodically stopping to pop ice bubbles.

By sticking with the intent to skate every day, and not being put off by the bad weather, we discovered a new species of experience—puddle skating. From the Harrisville Pond and others, Tara had learned the diplomacy of thin ice, and with this as a skill, I felt it was a right next step to try out sloppy and eerie conditions. When we skated over ice covered with an inch of water, the darkened water made a reflective mirror surface and we could watch ourselves glide along—a visual first in all my fifty years. Though only a few miles from home, it felt like we had stepped through the wardrobe into Narnia.

The previous spring, Tara had returned home from a multiday school outing that had included rock climbing and caving. The caving had been serious. They were underground for a number of hours, up to their waists in cold water, squirming through narrow passageways. The physical and psychic challenge had been just right for her at this point. She came home elated and struggled to explain her experience: *I feel so enlightened, like a new self, like there's new parts of myself I discovered. I never knew I could do that stuff. You don't know even how to explore those places, and then chances come and you actually get to do it. It opens up a whole new world, like a cavern of darkness that someone has shone a light on. I knew I could bike and run, but I never knew how wild my world was, right here in my own backyard of New England.*

Notice her analogy between light being shone on the darkness of the cavern and light being shone on the unexplored parts of her self. The parallels between outward exploration and inward explorations are particularly salient for adolescents. The Native Americans went wandering in the wilderness in search of a vision and a name; they sought an understanding of their own personal gifts and their unique mission. They strove to shed light on their inner lives. These skating explorations, these encounters with ice in all forms, constitute my palate of personal wisdom. A tattooing of the soul. For her, I seek a kind of indelible body knowledge of inner and outer places that will always be with her.

Looking Back: Taking the Plunge

Right here, in our own backyard of New England, we have enjoyed a third wild encounter with iciness. Cold water. In my own adolescence, I passionately consumed Ian Fleming novels, later popularized in the James Bond movies. The books were somewhat less glitzy than the movies have become, with more of a literate spy quality, like John Le Carré novels, or at least it seemed that way to me. For many male teens, the sophisticated secret agent served as a fantasy role model. I was no exception. One of James Bond's rituals was to complete his morning shower with an icy denouement. The quick switch from hot to cold water trained his heart to acclimate to the kinds of shock that spies had to be prepared for. I was hooked. I'd never drive an Aston Martin or have his rugged good looks, but I too could endure cold showers.

From there, my taste for cold water plunges evolved. Glacial lakes at 11,000 feet in the Kootenai Range in British Columbia, mid-January saunas where we had to chop through two feet of ice to make a plunge hole. I don't know if it created lightning-quick reflexes, or improved my chances of survival in a battle of wits with Dr. No, but it made me feel fully alive, like my whole body was sucking on a Halls eucalyptus drop. Whenever I travel, I try to find the local swimming hole, so I can baptize myself in the character of the local landscape. Only then do I feel as if I've arrived.

With my children, I think it started on Cape Cod. The cape at the end of May is like skiing on Tuesdays. Usually perfect conditions, devoid of traffic and clutter, an appealing emptiness. And the water is spy cold. When the kids were young, we'd take them out of school and go for two weeks. And how can you be on Cape Cod without swimming? The range of bodies of water provided a perfect training ground. By Memorial Day, the shallower kettle-hole ponds in Wellfleet had warmed up to near sixty degrees. We started there, then moved on to the bay beaches in Truro. Catch the incoming tide warmed by the wide tidal flats, and the water could be quite balmy. Do a first immersion in the child-friendly, knee-deep waters and then move out to water temperatures in the mid-fifties. Then, on the first really warm day, off to Newcomb Hollow or Long Nook on the Atlantic. The precipitous dune cliff and the deep green ocean waves provide the appropriate dramatic setting for taking the plunge into the forty-four-degree brine. And it didn't count unless you got your head wet.

Now it's a tradition. As soon as we arrive we zip down to Ryder Beach on Cape Cod Bay, usually in the late afternoon, and take a swim. It doesn't matter what the weather's like, we go in. A couple of years ago, we crested the dunes on that first afternoon in the teeth of a squall. Hard southwesterly wind-driven drizzle, good-sized waves for the bay, and a thick bog of every kind of seaweed imaginable out for about thirty feet. True gluck. I was ready to pass. The kids wouldn't think of it, and we had a blast draping gloppy algaes all over our bodies. When I arrived this year without them to write for a few days, I went in despite the bleak grayness, because I knew it would be the first thing they'd ask me on the phone.

The challenge of cold-water swimming has evolved into swimming in strange and odd places. On Isle au Haut in Maine, having internally mastered the seaweed yuck factor, we pioneered tide-pool swimming. Water shoes help. In Mexico we leaped fifteen feet down into a cenote named the Temple of Doom. This was formed where the surface limestone had collapsed into an underground river. The opening was about forty feet across and the lip of stone was overhung, so the pool underneath was much bigger than the opening. And you had to time your jump so as to miss the large bats that flew back and forth below you. Once you were down in the pool you peered back into the inky darkness of a circular cave and were thankful for the rickety ladder that led back up into sunlight. The water wasn't cold, but it sure was creepy, and I was proud of my children's gumption.

At home in New Hampshire, the cold factor has evolved into stretching the swimming, or more appropriately, dipping season as far as possible in both directions. No wet suits allowed. A few years ago we collected March on a really hot day after Eli and I had gone skiing. We got home, picked up Tara and Jereka, and made a beeline for Silver Lake. The heat spell had created an opening of about fifteen feet between the shore and the foot of ice still covering the lake, just enough for us to get wet in. We collected December, this past year, on the fourth or fifth, just before all that elegant black ice formed. It was one of those odd, global-warming days in the low sixties, and I was disappointed I couldn't leave work early to get home for a dip. I was carried along when Tara and Eli still wanted to forge ahead. At night, in December.

Can you anticipate the punch line? It was winter vacation week, a few days after the double-diamond challenge at Sugarbush. Another dreary day of slush and mud-splattered snow. As soon as I got home, Tara met me at the door . . .

"Guess what Daddy?" she said gleefully, her hair a bit damp, her eyes bright, her cheeks flushed with color. "I got February! I went back to the gorge, Gwinna (the dog) and I. And above the dam, where the water was melted out right before the spillway, I went for a swim, all the way under."

"But it was barely above freezing. Weren't you uncomfortable?" I exclaimed.

"It wasn't even that cold, really, and Gwinna was there to save me. I didn't even bring a towel."

She had raised the bar herself, and jumped over it, with no audience but her own inner eye. She was proving herself ready to go out in the world, set the goal, measure the risks, and pull it off on her own. It's exactly what adolescents need, this internalized sense of their own authority. She was going underwater, but not underground. Only January is left.

January 8, 2000. The last weekend before school starts again. We've returned from skiing for a couple of days. Still no snow, and the ice remains unblemished. Don't look a gift horse in the mouth. I envision the consummation of all our preparations—the Nubanusit and Spoonwood Loop. Nubanusit, the largest lake in our area, is deep, so it's often the last lake to freeze completely. You can start on the shallow end of Nubanusit, skate a mile, walk the portage trail to Spoonwood, a protected wilderness pond. Then you skate the length of Spoonwood, clomp over the dam at the far end, and get back onto an arm of Nubanusit. Then it's out and around onto the wide, deep part of the lake and eventually, hopefully, back to the starting point. Since Nubanusit doesn't ever completely freeze before the snow flies, this eight-mile skating loop is mostly a long-distance dream. In fact, I don't know anybody who's done it.

For Tara and I, this is a quantum leap up. While our other forays have been one- or two-hour outings, this is more of an expedition. Breaking through in marshy, shallow water is a pain, but not really dangerous. Deep water presents more of a life-and-death situation. And eight miles requires endurance—possible foot cramps, muscle fatigue, and for me, back pain. Tara understands the seriousness and makes the commitment. Tara recalls:

On this beautiful morning, we decide to attempt the loop around Nubanusit and Spoonwood, and the only thing stopping us from completing it would be the thickness of the ice. We got there, laced our skates, and completed the first mile within fifteen minutes. The ice was perfect for endless gliding, and we both thought, "Well, this will be a shorter trip than we figured." We crossed the canoe trail on our skates, skating little frozen puddles on the way. As we started skating up Spoonwood, I felt this amazing sense of freedom. We had left behind the icefishers and snowmobiles and now danced across the ice as if we were the only living creatures on this brisk, sunlit, winter morning. As we got down toward the end of Spoonwood, we began to experience the first sections of thin ice. We avoided it, moving with care, but no real worry.

Well, not quite. There's a big swath of open water to our left at the end of the pond with little wavelets kicking up in the wind. On the right, there's a rocky peninsula with a channel of water between the ice and the shore. There's a solid fifty feet of ice between the two bands of open water and we constantly check the ice thickness, but my pulse rate surges as we tread lightly across the ice bridge. Here, we're over deep water. We spread out with me going first, knowing that if the ice holds my weight, it will be okay for Tara. We talk about reasonable risk, and I suggest we are starting to push up against the edge. We head for shore, take off our skates and hike the last quarter mile until we're over the dam and on to a solidly frozen lobe of Nubanusit.

As we move across Nubanusit again, we did start to get a little nervous, because the ice was thin and getting thinner. We inched along at the pace of a snail until it got too thin to go any further. It was about an inch thick, and that is nowhere near thick enough, so we decided to turn back.

Rounding the bend onto the wide part of Nubanusit, my skin started to crawl. The ice is as black and smooth as a moonless night. And there's something spooky about the silence. I keep expecting to hear little hints of cracking, or that rolling thunder of ice expanding, but there's nothing. I wonder if the ice isn't even thick enough to make noise. We stay close to the shore, but it drops off deeply here, so it'll be full immersion if we go through. It's getting harder to check ice depth visually because it's hard to see where the ice ends and the water begins. I sit down to use the technique of kicking the rear end of my figure skate blade through the ice. One chop and water erupts through the fracture. The ice is barely an inch thick. I swallow gingerly. Creepy, anticipatory horror movie music emerges from the crowded spruces along the shoreline, like the shark is about to burst through the placid surface. Reluctantly, we retreat, spacing ourselves widely for the half mile back to dependable ice. I'm happy to be free of those little shivers up and down my spine.

We were both disappointed, but it did not ruin the overall experience. We stopped when we had about two miles to go. We built a little campfire, spread out a picnic, roasted sausages and peppers, and ate while sunlight filtered through the branches upon our faces. When we got back to the starting point and were talking to the ice fishermen, they mentioned that the half of the loop we weren't able to skate was open water. It was definitely a good decision to turn back. We ended up skating about six miles today and it hardly felt like two. Skating is a wonderful way to travel. Too bad Venice isn't a city on ice.

At lunch, we stretch out in the leaves, an odd combination of January temperatures and October dryness. I talk to Tara about "the wisdom of not doing," Freeman Tilden's term for projects that are better off left undone. On Harrisville Pond, it was right to take the risk and keep going, to honor the original intent and make it way up into the marshy interior. Courage is good. Today, it was right to turn back. Humility is good. For everything, there is a season. Store these memories of ice as guideposts for future dilemmas. Should I take this job? Should I stay up all night to finish this assignment? Should I trust this guy? You're developing the skills to make those decisions.

Carefree, we stride back up the expanse of Spoonwood, leaving long, symmetrical blade marks on the slate surface. At the peninsula where Tara and I camped for a couple of nights three or four years ago, we recall the good diving spots, sketching the canoe in the late afternoon light, the hike over to Elephant Rock where we stuffed our mouths chipmunk-full of blueberries. A bit beyond, we stop at a trail of feathers, wind-drifted as far as the eye can follow. The remnants of a grouse taken by a coyote perhaps. Each downy feather frozen delicately on a satin backdrop, like our string of skating afternoons.

Kindling the Spark

A couple of weeks ago I dropped Tara off at Yankee Lanes to meet Colin for her first real date. And our last ski day for the winter didn't work out because Tara wanted to go snowboarding with a bunch of friends. Just in the past few months, we've started to talk about the necessity of a second phone line because Tara is talking to her friends endlessly. Irony and eye shadow are more common on her face. She's not around on weekends as much, and we're all starting to miss her a bit. But she's incredibly helpful around the house, she makes a mean guacamole, and it's really fun to talk to her about presidential politics and the morality of environmental pollution. She's growing up.

My wife and I consider it valuable to honor each new developmental shift for our children. Our goals with Tara's transition into adolescence are to honor the child she's been, celebrate the person she's becoming, and utilize the new openness and thirst at puberty to pass on some wisdom about right livelihood. Last summer, Tara participated in a Coming of Age for Young Women program offered by Kroka Expeditions in Brattleboro, Vermont—six girls and two women leaders tucked into an isolated campsite near a lake in the Green Mountain wilderness. At departure, the leaders had each girl and parent hold opposite ends of a length of yarn to signify their connections. Then the yarn was snipped—a symbol of separation—and each parent was told to hold on to the yarn and bring it back at journey's end.

The girls endured hardship and were securely held by the leaders and one another. Each day they created a different ritual experience. On a frame of saplings, they wove the walls that became the container for a Moon Lodge ritual where they learned the importance of giving and receiving. Another day they immersed themselves in the mud and muck of a bog, the slime hardened on their skins, and then they walked half a mile to wash off in the cool waters of a clear lake. The grime and refreshment of adult life.

One late afternoon they huddled under a tarp on top of their life preservers as a violent microburst thunderstorm ripped across southern Vermont and New Hampshire. As I sat in my office in the odd green light and torrents of rain, I felt pangs of anxiety, and the mixed sadness and joy of her independence.

On their last night, they did a traditional sweat—"one of the hardest things I've ever done," she said later. And they talked about who they had been as children, who they were becoming, and what they had learned from their parents. At the ceremonial reentry, their laughter and stories let us parents glimpse the community of young womanhood that had emerged during the week. The girls' yarn had been woven into something new to signify how they had taken the thread of connection with their parents and woven it into something beautiful. All the girls wrote journals in their personal places of power during the week. In her final entry, Tara said:

Looking up at the sky through the foliage, I realize that my life is a truly precious and beautiful thing. I want to kindle its spark, bring it to flame, and, if I can, bring it to a roaring fire of happiness. Which will not be stomped out or extinguished in any unnatural way, so that it may burn down to the last ember, which will then quietly, happily slip into the blissful and endless sleep of Death.

All the encounters with iciness—difficult skiing, exploratory skating, cold-water immersions—have been part of kindling Tara's spark. The harsh coldness on the outside necessitates the fire of inner determination. The steep slope makes the muscles burn. Facing death means embracing life.

There's at least one more component to the rite of passage for Tara. She's gone into the wilderness with a group of young women, and she and I have faced ice together. Last week, at dinner, we discussed her approaching solo experience and the preparations she'll have to undergo to get ready. Next summer, I'll paddle her out to the campsite on the peninsula on Spoonwood and bid her farewell. She'll be sung to sleep by the loons. Next morning, she'll swim the length of Spoonwood, a long personal adventure. The long swim is a Nootka tradition in British Columbia. The initiates are dropped off out in the ocean as girls and emerge on the beach as women. As she slices down the empty green lake, I hope her fire is kindled with her memories of *dancing across the ice as if we were the only living creatures on that brisk, sunlit, winter morning.*

STEPHEN J. LYONS

The Eagles of Beauty Bay

Ten bald eagles, resembling giant black and white kites, cast themselves back and forth in the updrafts between Beauty Bay and Mineral Ridge in an eastern inlet of Lake Coeur d'Alene. Their seven-foot wingspans never waver from steady flight and their ivory heads—more precisely, their yellow eyes, which see eight times sharper than our own—notice every move we make from the road.

Tamarack and grand fir comb the mist that hovers over the bay. It's mid-afternoon and the eagles are through feeding on the dying kokanee. The eagles will slowly circle back to their favorite roosting trees, dropping the half-eaten carcasses of the lake salmon to the forest floor where giant, scavenging ravens continue the biological balancing act while beetles and ants wait their turn in the food chain. When the salmon are depleted the eagles will turn their attention to thinning out old or sick ducks. Easy pickings. Not surprisingly, no ducks are to be seen. On the lake the word is out: The eagles are back.

No need for the Audubon bird guide today. We can easily look across the small bay and identify five eagles roosting in a tree. We look for white heads, white tail feathers, and a regal, somehow patriotic attitude we foolishly attach to them. For eagles care nothing about our red, white, black, and blue attitudes. Our pomp and dire circumstances. They are hungry. That's all.

Kokanee in the lake live four years, then come back here to spawn and die. I can only speculate, but I think the fish know exactly what they need to do every day of their 1,400-day life cycle. How I envy them.

We have driven more than three hours on this low-light, overcast day in late December through the lake country of northern Idaho to see the annual bald eagle migration. We brought peanut butter and raisin sandwiches on freshly baked sourdough bread; small carrots that snap in our mouths like dry willow; a thermos of cocoa; and large slices of walnut-pumpkin cake dusted with powdered sugar that falls with each bite like sticky snow onto our sweaters. This is food to be eaten outdoors.

We are not alone. Car after car pulls into a nearby campground and families get out and walk leisurely along the road—binoculars and children in tow. From the looks of clothing, age, and make of cars (or "rigs" as Westerners call any combustible engine vehicle), the entire social strata is here. Logger and lawyer. Masseuse and machinist. Farmer and flight attendant. Judging by the smiles and conversation, there seems to be complete consensus. Finally. Today, everyone in northern Idaho is pro-eagle.

How could we not love these eagles? If we cannot love these birds, we cannot love anything. If we forget to connect their lives of wildness to our own, we are ultimately lost. Perhaps it's too late on a large scale to teach an interest and respect for the natural world. But on a one-to-one, father-to-daughter scale, anything remains possible. I have lived with the proof for fourteen years, and she stands beside me today.

Rose is less interested in the eagles than she would have been a couple of years ago. Separation is not far off and her own identity is emerging, an identity that may not include bird watching or hiking through the icy wind of Lake Coeur d'Alene. I know she'd rather be with her friends than with parents and bald eagles, listening to the rock band Counting Crows instead of counting eagles with Dad. Still, there is something here she will take away from this afternoon although she does not know that yet. Someday, no matter where she is, she will remember birds, pine trees, December light; the distinctive musty odor of ancient lakes, the narrow roads that wind past the living rooms and kitchens in the hard-nosed, blue-collar Idaho timber towns like Harrison and Emida, where the order of each and every day is an unglamorous form of gritty survival.

If, up to this point, I have done my parenting job well, she might recall these reference points of landscape and maybe realize her own place in this green world of canyons, five-fingered ferns, river rocks, forest canopy, and eagles. The memory of this particular day might surface in a dream or arrive in the form of a certain slant of light, the scent of pine tree, a spoken word, a photograph, the texture of a piece of clothing, or a passage from a book.

My parenting is in a new, unenviable stage. During these teenage years I see myself in a struggle for the very soul of my daughter. Her attention is elsewhere as she searches for her own ideals. Age-old values found in nature and the hearth of home; the celebration of the humbly ordinary are mocked and opposed by the noise of our billion-dollar image industry that promotes ridicule, accumulation, promiscuity, and transience. How can a parent's voice emerge through the constant barrage of flashy, digital images perfectly choreographed to rock and roll and rap? How do I compete with a de-evolving culture that promotes passive attention and loneliness, but never a serious emotional commitment? Nature and the biological kingdom have few advocates. It's up to me to promote this world to Rose.

Reliable role models of parents, grandparents, community and religious leaders (the honest ones), and teachers have been co-opted by the empty sound bites of illiterate athletes, spaced-out "musicians," and millionaire actors with impeccable bridgework. Overnight success without hard work is the message of the day in the videos, ads, and movies that assault my daughter. The one overriding question in American culture remains: "What's it like to be rich and famous and beautiful?"

How conservative I must seem to Rose. Papa with his field guides, maps, binoculars, acoustic music, who, at the drop of a word can rant and rave on every subject from beer commercials and karaoke to lotteries and militias. During one struggle, I suggest canoeing. She makes a face. Let's go look at flowers on Kamiak? She tells me I'm old. Her bedroom door closes. Sometimes, late at night, I hear her push the plastic buttons on her Walkman (the worst contraption ever invented), followed by the industrial buzz of Nirvana, Hole, and Green Day. Recently, she proudly quoted a friend, "Nature is boring. Nothing happens." Exactly my point.

Humility. That's one quality I'm trying to teach Rose today in this icy corner of Idaho. The idea is to show her an alternative to this media madness and lonely egotism, a place where she can hear her own internal message. Rose will eventually struggle through the noisy clamor of this culture, the coming of age, and draw her own conclusions about the worth of both worlds.

Have I adequately prepared her for life's fights? I review my mental list of axioms. The final list of fatherly advice: Clip coupons and always buy generic. Memorize some lines of poetry. Learn to play a musical instrument. Exercise, but never weigh yourself. Make a lot of money and then give it all away. Learn the names of flowers, plants, and birds. Sleep with the windows open. Recycle. Eat out only in small-town cafes where the waitress is also the cook, bartender, and day-care coordinator. Volunteer in the community. Cultivate solitude. Forgive yourself. Bring your own bag to the grocery store. Never date a man that sports a National Rifle Association sticker on his rig. Don't run the water needlessly when brushing your teeth. Use less of everything. Hug a tree. Don't spit. Be of good cheer.

I sneak a look at my daughter. Behind her five foot, eleven inch frame I see the eagles circling, creating a halo above her. She has certainly come a long way since those early days full of divorce and fear five years ago. She is an outgoing ninth grader, surrounded by lifelong friends—her support group. No longer immersed in full-time introspection, Rose plays volleyball and sings in the alto section of the Moscow Junior High Select Choir. At a recent volleyball game, her mother, also sitting in the bleachers watching Rose run around the court full of confidence, screaming encouragement at teammates, turned to me and said with astonishment, "She's normal!"

I think of how our first trip after divorce unraveled our family, and how hard it was just to get out of bed each morning and make coffee. In our search for a new place in the world we trusted in the feeling that comes from trumpeter swans in flight and the sudden burst of an antelope across our path. The less dramatic was equally important; simple tasks of putting up a tent, sitting on river rocks, hiking, boiling water, and taking the time to identify hawks, songbirds, and the mica-encrusted shelters of the caddis fly. For a while we stopped talking. And with all our collected might, we ran until all we could hear was wind in our ears. Now we have stopped running.

We began to name the world around us. In the white pine forest north of Moscow we came across the ghostly brown parasitic Indian pipe flower, devoid of chlorophyll and leaves, that gathers nutrients from nearby green plants. We learn of its family, wintergreen, with familial connections to pinedrops and candysticks. On the northeastern slope of Kamiak Butte, in early spring, grows the fairy slipper, or calypso, of the orchid family, which was named, according to Audubon's *Field Guide to North American Wildflowers*, "for the sea nymph Calypso of Homer's *Odyssey*, who detained the willing Odysseus on his return from Troy; like Calypso, the plant is beautiful and prefers secluded haunts." Indeed, the fairy slipper is a skittish orchid that hides under ferns in the moist parts of the forest.

Fairy slipper leads to another thought, a connection to the opposite of the flower spectrum, the gaudy Indian paintbrush, a member of the figwort or snapdragon family and a partial parasite, with relatives like the monkeyflower and purple Chinese houses. Not shy at all, paintbrush prefers the open, exposed slopes, where it shows off its fireworks of colors in reds and oranges.

Preferences. Personalities. Temperaments that run the gamut. Like all families.

Maybe these discoveries have to do with focus and awe, that our own problems can be overshadowed by simply stepping outside and paying close attention. We gather strength from a world that demonstrates power in forms that make our crude efforts puny in comparison. And at the time Rose and I were unconnected to family, landscape took us in.

Divorce and loss has brought us a special form of closeness we might not have ever attained otherwise. It also brought us a type of emotional street smarts. Poet Tess Gallagher describes it best as a "refugee mentality . . . you learn to be industrious toward the prospect of love and shelter. You know both are fragile and that stability must lie with you or it is nowhere. You make a home of yourself." Broken family? At first. But not now. Stronger? Definitely. Wiser? Rose is. Whether I am is open for lively debate.

Sundays Rose returns to her mother and stepfather. I am never prepared. It is always an awkward emotional transition to have your child for one week, then lose her for the next. To never know how dramatic to make your goodbye. Sometimes before she leaves, bags of clothes and a tangle of shoes, books, and tapes stacked up at the door, we play volleyball in the backyard. Over and over again I serve hard line drives to her and she gracefully returns the serves with artful digs. With each return of serve the heaviness lifts as the physical activity overtakes the mental gymnastics of assessing this court-mandated separation.

Then we load up the car and drive to her mother and stepfather's house in Deary. It's a route that takes us through the best of this Palouse country. East from Moscow, fields give way to patches of tamarack and fir, with the occasional aspen grove and the cul-de-sacs of too much new California ranch-style housing. Along the way, Paradise Ridge, Tomer Butte, and Buffalo Hump rise to the south; the wheat, dry pea, and rapeseed fields are in various stages of ebb and flow and color combinations, as are the many varieties of flowers and plants, such as wild roses, lupine, and yellow peas. At Joel, a mere trace cluster of houses and trailers, a silver grain elevator is the tallest structure around. The road curves sharply, and to the north are beautiful panoramic views of Moscow Mountain, with its smaller twin towers descending off the Palouse range to the west and eastern Washington.

After passing Carlson's orchard and used car lot, a rush of cold air hits us no matter what time of year and we descend Driscoll Ridge, past

Clint's auction business and antique shop on the right, situated in a dark, northern exposure where the last patches of the previous winter's snow can always be found. Then the smell of cedar from the mill yard, the combination minimart-laundromat-car wash ("Power Ball, 30 Million, lattes 99¢, Smoky Joe sale"), the wide main street of Troy, usually littered with logging slash; the new library and post office, the general store where locals can still buy groceries on a tab, the Troy Phone Company, the Troy Tavern, the ubiquitous video store operating out of a converted gas station, then a sharp turn east out of town over the rarely used Burlington Northern Railroad tracks. This drive through town takes two minutes.

On the other side of Troy the country gets steeper and the croplands give way to larger stretches of forestland, with ponds and marshes. The sky opens up. We share the road with chip trucks, grain trucks, horse trailers, skunks and badgers, shiny shards of mica, belching pickups with gun racks loaded with firewood from the Clearwater National Forest, road graders, road kills, deer, boats, kestrels and northern harriers, and house trailers. Green signs appear in front of homesteads: "This family supported by timber dollars." We pass the Spring Valley turnoff, two gravel pits, and dirt roads that lead to three clay pits. There's the Troy and Deary Gun Club, Zimmerman's Logging with the gigantic wooden logger carving in front of the office, then front yards full of pinto horses and automobile husks, ragged outbuildings, and red barns. We dip down Dry Ridge, over the seasonal Bear Creek, and up again past the small sign leading to Zion Cemetery. ("A good one," Rose says, looking out the window. She should know. She's been to every one in the county.) Finally, after twenty-six miles, Potato Hill— Spud Hill to everyone in northern Idaho—leans into view, and we shift down, passing the Deary sewage pond, the Washington, Idaho, and Montana Railroad tracks, to Rose's country home just off the highway.

We say our goodbyes in the yard—my well-practiced lines: "Call me this week, OK?" I find Rose's eyes, then a hug, and we go our separate ways. Driving back to Moscow, I think, "This makes absolutely no sense at all." It's just one of many self-defeating thoughts that I'll spend the next six days digesting.

After I return home, I often look for solace in the form of a photograph on my desk of Rose from one of our camping trips. Within the silver frame, she stands on a tumble of giant, lichen-splashed rocks on the shore of the Selway River. Moving up the valley behind her is an early summer shower, the kind of weather Rose was born in and still thrives in. Her long hair rises as the barometer drops; arms crossed, long fingers relaxed. Her dark eyes stare back, unwavering. Her mouth is closed, set in the slightest of smiles. Her age is hard to guess. If you came across this girl you would immediately take a step back. You would tell her only the truth. You would hear the distant thunder rumbling somewhere over the craggy peaks of the Bitterroots and associate her forever with ancient river rocks and gathering clouds of electricity. And strength.

She looks back at you. Unblinking. Determined. She is saying, to all of us, I am ready for anything.

SCOTT RUSSELL SANDERS

Mountain Music IV

On a sultry August afternoon in the Smoky Mountains, a year after our quarrel in the Rockies, Jesse and I fell to talking about God. It was Jesse who brought up this grandest of all subjects, and he did most of the talking, because we were climbing a steep trail with loaded packs and he was the only one with a supply of breath.

"I remember when I was little," he said, "and it dawned on me one day that everything alive was filled with God."

"You must have been eight," I said, huffing. "Maybe nine."

"And then I realized that the grass was alive, and the dirt was alive, and suddenly I was afraid of setting my foot down because I'd be walking on God. I remember we were playing baseball in Bryan Park."

"You were chasing a fly ball. Then you just stopped."

"I stood there in the outfield, calling you. I was so scared."

"Sprained ankle, I figured. Or a bee sting."

"You carried me all the way home."

"And you were a load, let me tell you." I grunted, took a few more panting steps, then halted. "You must have weighed as much as this pack."

Jesse turned on me those gleaming brown eyes that have always made me think of Ruth. "Want a break?" he asked.

"Good idea." I wiped a forearm across my slick face. "It's not that I'm tired. I just don't want to wear you out on the first day."

We rested on the trunk of a fallen hemlock, sharing a bottle of water and a handful of raisins. Butterflies lilted past us, heading up the slope, hundreds of them in dozens of colors, feeding on the gangly flowers that grew in the rare openings along the trail. The valley of the Little Tennessee River, where we had parked the car, lay a few miles behind us, and the campsite we were aiming for lay a few miles farther on. Rain had followed us all the way south from Indiana on our drive that morning, and here in the mountains, a ranger told us, it had been raining for most of a week. The gray sky threatened more rain, but so far it was holding back. Creeks rushed down the slope on both sides of the trail, enveloping us in murmurs and mist. I drew in lungfuls of dank air.

"It really freaked me out," Jesse said, "to realize that God was in the grass, in the dirt, in bugs on the sidewalk, and in the mashed potatoes on my plate. Either God was everywhere, or he was nowhere. He couldn't just be inside a church or a book. He couldn't be trapped just inside human beings, or even just on earth."

"What do you think about all of that now?" I asked.

"Obviously I got over the fear of walking." Jesse leaned forward on the log and glanced down at his mud-caked boots, which had carried him around Europe earlier in the summer, and on previous treks through mountains, gorges, creeks, and forests in half a dozen states. "And I lost my confidence in talking about God," he added. What he had not lost, he went on to say, was his feeling that a great and mysterious power works through all things; he still wondered how we might contact that power and where it might be leading us.

On this journey, by mutual consent, Jesse was leading us. The trip had been his idea, a last chance to stretch his legs and sleep on dirt before he started college. I'd asked if he wanted to bring along a couple of his hiking buddies, but he insisted that the two of us go alone. "I feel like I haven't really talked with you in months," he said. He planned the meals, packed the gear, studied the maps. When I offered to help, he shrugged his big shoulders and answered, "No problem. I've got it under control." He was familiar with the Smokies, had even hiked this mountain loop twice before with friends. In every way except age, Jesse was the veteran here and I was the tenderfoot. Sensing his need to play the leader, I honored this reversal of roles.

"You figure we'll reach the campsite before dark?" I asked him.

"For sure. The trail levels out pretty soon, runs through a stretch of pines, crosses the creek three or four times. Then we'll be there. You ready to go for it?"

"Ready as I'll ever be."

At the rapid swinging pace that suited his long legs he set out up the trail, which zigzagged along switchbacks and through stands of ash and oak, sassafras and maple, hemlock and tulip poplar. The temperature fell as we climbed. Sure enough, the muddy track soon leveled out, then ran on through a plantation of pines. But I lost my breath anyway, humping along under the weight of my pack. So I mainly listened while Jesse told me that he wondered if humans might be poised to break through into a new level of consciousness. He wondered if maybe that's what lay behind all our troubles. Maybe God was urging us toward a new vision of our place in the world, a vision more tender and peaceful and spiritual.

In his words I could hear echoes of the Buddha and Jesus and mystics the world over. But I didn't say so, not wanting to rub the freshness from his insight.

"We need to be more loving," he said. "It's like our hearts need to catch up with our brains and hands." He trudged on a few paces in silence, then stopped, as abruptly as on that long ago day in the park when he had stood paralyzed in the grass by the fear of treading on God. He swung around to face me. "Do you believe we can change? That we're not stuck in this dead-end way of thinking?"

The intensity in his face and voice demanded the truth. So I considered carefully before answering. "Yes I do."

Jesse gazed at me for a moment, no longer as a boy studying his father but as one man testing another. Then relief spread through him visibly, softening his face, relaxing his body. "That makes two of us."

"Enough to start a movement," I suggested.

"Or join one."

"You mean other people?"

"I mean other people," he said. "And whatever else may be heading in the right direction."

With about an hour of daylight left, we reached our campsite in a cove at the junction of three creeks. As in the Rockies a year before, so here in the Smokies, every stream was swollen, and the purr of tumbling water rubbed over us. We laid out our gear on a poncho and pitched our tent on the damp ground. The rain still held off, yet everything was already soaked, including the dead branches we gathered for a fire. The dampness must have been perennial, because the trees were clad in moss and lichens, not only down among the roots but well above our heads. Ferns curled up everywhere from rotting logs the color of bricks, mushrooms thrust pale thumbs up through matted leaves, and rhododendrons arched over the creeks. In the gathering darkness, tree frogs began to call, soon loudly enough to rival the racket of hustling water.

In spite of the dampness, I managed to get a fire started, and to keep it going with a steady flame. Jesse cooked burritos on our tiny gas stove, frying hamburger and stirring in peppers and onions and seasoning. He insisted on doing all the cooking, not only for this meal but for the whole trip, so I volunteered to wash dishes. This amused him, because he and his buddies never bothered with cleaning up, figuring that grease and grot were essential to the woods experience. After we ate, Jesse was even more amused that I stripped off all my sweaty clothes and waded into the froth of a creek to bathe. He kidded me about going soft from my indoor life. I kidded him in turn about how black bears are drawn to the stink of unbathed hikers. The truth was that I cared less about getting clean than about lying naked in the rush of water. The creek was cold and I shivered when I stood up dripping in the mountain air.

It felt good to sit beside the fire while the gray sky turned black. Jesse read *The Moor's Last Sigh*, by Salman Rushdie, and I wrote in my notebook, both of us tilting our pages to catch the flickering light. I kept glancing at him, his face so absorbed, the gingery beard glinting on his jaw, the shoulder-length blond hair drawn back in a pony-tail, the fathomless brown eyes. On our drive from Indiana, he had told me that the summer of tramping in Europe had restored his love of reading. He'd lost his way in high school, he said, lost any clear sense of why he was getting those straight A's. During his travels that summer, bumping into other students, sleeping on borrowed floors, riding all-night trains to ancient cities that were brand-new to him, slouching through museums, reading novels in sidewalk cafes, he'd rediscovered the point of learning. And what is that? I asked. "It's fun," he answered. "It enlarges your life, and it prepares you to do some good in the world."

Reading now by firelight, Jesse looked up from his book every once in a while to recall something about those weeks in Europe.

"I'd meet strangers," he said at one point, "maybe in a youth hostel or train station, or crossing a street, and they'd stare at me as though they knew me somehow. We'd find a language we could talk—English, usually, or maybe French, or some fractured Spanish—and I would ask a few questions. And before I knew it, people I'd never seen before were telling me their life stories, and it was like I'd run into lost brothers or sisters." Now he figured that everyone he met had something to teach him, if only about what to avoid on his path through life.

A while later, Jesse asked me what I was scribbling in my notebook.

"What happened today, more or less," I answered.

"For your book on hope?"

"Some of it may wind up there."

"Including what I say?"

"Could be. Do you mind?"

He pondered that a spell, rubbing the bristle on his chin. Sap sizzled in the coals. Finally he said, "It's okay, so long as I don't come off as a fool kid."

"You're the hero," I told him. "One of the heroes, anyway."

He looked at me hard to make sure I wasn't teasing. "Must be a strange book."

Light rain eventually drove us into the tent, where we lay shoulder to shoulder, with our jeans rolled up under our heads for pillows. Within minutes Jesse was asleep. Too tired for sleep, I lay there listening. No wind, no creak of limbs, no grumble of engines, only water song and frog song and our entwined breaths.

Jesse had changed a great deal, and so had I, in the year since we'd quarreled in Big Thompson Canyon and rafted down the river and turned back in the face of lightning over Thunder Lake. I'd spent the year trying to see the world through his eyes, through Eva's eyes, through the eyes of my students, while working on this book. Whatever my words might eventually mean to these young people, the effort to speak of hope had renewed my own courage. Meanwhile Jesse finished high school, decided to stay in our hometown for college, grieved over the death of his best friend's father, saw other friends succumb to dope or drink or depression, and then for six weeks he'd backpacked around Europe, time enough for him to savor his newfound independence, miss his family, and take on responsibility for his life.

I didn't understand all of the changes, in him or in me, but on the whole they seemed to me blessings. We'd become friends once more. There was an ease in our talk and work together that I had not felt with him for half a dozen years. I could groan over the country music he played on the car radio as we drove south, and instead of taking offense he would laugh. And he could tell me to chill out when I worried aloud about hillsides of pines in the Smokies turning brown, and I felt no urge to lecture him about acid rain. I still could not turn off my fathering mind, but I could turn down the volume, quiet the fretful voice, and enjoy the company of my grown son, without worrying constantly, as I had the year before, that at any moment our voices might begin clashing like swords.

We woke inside a cloud. Trees loomed around us like ghostly columns, their upper branches veiled in white. The creeks purred on, invisible, but the frogs had hushed.

"Where'd everything go?" Jesse muttered, then rolled over in his sleeping bag.

I lay there remembering a park sign we had come across the day before, which explained that three-quarters of the haze in the air that gave these mountains their name now comes from pollution, and only one-quarter from gases released by decaying matter. There was plenty of matter for decay in these old woods, in the leaf duff and downed logs and spongy soil.

I pulled on cold jeans and crawled from the tent and walked on stiff legs to filter drinking water from the nearest creek. Mist rode the current, wafting and spinning under the boughs of rhododendrons, their leaves dangling like green donkey's ears. Hearing a twig crack behind me, I turned, thinking it was Jesse, but it was a deer, coming to drink at the creek maybe ten paces from where I squatted. It looked to be a yearling doe, slender and neat. She stood with her forefeet close together and bent her muzzle to the water and the muscles in her neck rippled as she swallowed. Water had never seemed so good to me as it did while I watched her drink. Then I did hear Jesse, the tramp of his boots coming my way, and in the same instant the deer jerked her head up, pricked up her ears, spun around in one convulsive motion with white tail raised and bounded off noisily into the fog.

"Did you see the deer?" Jesse asked wonderingly as he drew close to me.

"Wasn't she a beauty?"

"For a second there I thought maybe it was a bear."

Jesse took over from me, pumping water through the filter into our plastic bottles, and as he worked he told about sighting bears on his previous trips into the Smokies. Once he and his two partners had swung around a bend in the trail, and there sat a mother and her cub, feeding on blackberries, sleek fur gleaming in the noonday sun. Jesse knew better than to crowd a cub, so he and his buddies just stood there while the bears ate with long red tongues and much blinking of shiny black eyes. It seemed the bears would never tire of berries, so eventually Jesse and his buddies circled out through the woods and rejoined the trail at a safe distance beyond.

"I'm dressed for them," he said, pointing at his chest.

He wore a clean white T-shirt from a Grateful Dead concert. The words on the front posed a question—WHAT DO YOU DO IF YOU MEET A BEAR IN THE WOOD?—and the back offered an answer: PLAY DEAD.

Despite the morning chill, his thick legs jutted out bare from cut-off jeans.

"Aren't you cold?" I asked.

"Not so long as I keep moving."

We tightened the caps on our water bottles. Every time I drank from mine that day I would think of the deer, and of how generous the world is to satisfy our thirst.

After a breakfast of omelets with green peppers, we broke camp and shouldered the packs and made our way uphill through cloud. The trees might have stopped ten feet above our heads, for all we could see of their branches, and only their bark and the nuts and acorns underfoot identified them as mostly oak and hickory. The trail was littered with broken stone, and the rootballs from fallen trees exposed the shattered bedrock that lay everywhere beneath thin soil, reminders that these were old, snaggle-toothed mountains, far older than the Rockies, and they had been eroding for three hundred million years.

Although it was August, prime vacation season in the Smokies, we had met no one on our hike the day before, and this day we met only a father and his two young daughters clumping downhill looking bedraggled. Jesse and I stepped back to let them pass. The girls' hair frizzed out beneath baseball caps and they peered up at us with glum expressions. The father paused long enough to say they had planned to stay longer, but every stitch of clothing they had with them was soaked through, and no prospect of drying out any time soon, so they were packing it in.

At midmorning we came to a grassy clearing that gave us a view of the sky, what there was of it, and we could see a hint of sun to the east like a single dim headlight on an idle train. By noon, when we stopped for lunch on the open crest of a mountain, the light had chugged on overhead but had grown no brighter, and the sky glowed a pale indigo. We shucked off our packs and hunched down on our spread-out ponchos and ate peanut butter sandwiches, breathing vapor. A few butterflies lolled past, their colors washed out, and they fed on thistles bleached white by cloud. We could see mist easing by on a wind too subtle for hearing. Even these few glimpses of the ghostly world came to us only because this mountain top was bare of trees, one of those openings in the Smokies known as balds. What originally kept the forest back, whether grazing long ago by deer and elk and even bison, or maybe fires lit by lightning or Cherokees, no one knows, but these openings show up on the earliest surveys of the mountains, from the 1820s, and now the Park Service works to keep them clear. Jesse had wanted to show me the panorama visible from this peak on a clear day, but on this day of swirling whiteness he could only describe for me what I might have seen.

"Sounds beautiful," I said when he had finished.

"It is," he agreed. "Way beyond words."

I washed down the last of my sandwich with some of the creek water I had shared with the deer, and then I left Jesse reading his novel while I went out to hunt for blueberries. After only a dozen paces I looked back and could barely make out his dark silhouette in the cottony air. Not wanting to lose sight of him, I traced out a slow circle with Jesse at the center. Moist grass lapped against my legs, and seedling pines, and cardinal flowers shimmering a dull red, until I came to a patch of low bushes covered with berries that looked in this vaporous air like silver beads. Even blanched of color they were blueberries, all right, as my tongue quickly told me. I picked less by sight than by touch, tilted a handful into my mouth, and savored the burst of tangy sweetness. I ate a second handful and a third, understanding why bears would not quit eating so long as the flavor stayed fresh. Thought of bears made me keep glancing up as I picked, on the lookout for a burly shape heaving toward me through the mist.

The fourth handful I carried back to Jesse, who sat as I had left him, with the book balanced on his lifted knees. He accepted the blueberries with thanks and began popping them into his mouth a few at a time, never taking his eyes from the page. Again I circled away from him, this time with our two drinking cups, and when I returned both cups were heaped with berries.

"You leave any for the poor bears?" Jesse asked.

"A few," I assured him.

We sat there among the drifting clouds munching the tart berries, and I could not tell whether the ones I ate or the ones my son ate gave me more pleasure.

The campsite for our second night was a favorite of Jesse's from previous trips, on a flat ridgetop among old trees growing wide apart. Before setting up he led me around the place eagerly, as if it were a haunt of his childhood, showing me a huge log the color of bone, where he liked to stretch out, a heap of windblown gray birches where he always gathered firewood, a spring oozing over mossy ledges into a fern-fringed pool where he drew his water, a clearing where he watched the stars.

We would see no stars that night, nor much of anything else during the day, for the dense cloud shut off vision at a distance of fifty feet or so. Jesse and I worked along as though wrapped in fleece. Practiced at making camp, we hardly spoke as we pitched the shivering blue tent upwind from the stone ring of the fire pit, strung a line to hang out our wet socks and shirts in air as damp as they were, then rigged my poncho among four scrawny trees to make an awning against the rain that was sure to come. While Jesse cobbled together a rough bench by lashing dead limbs together, I ranged about gathering firewood. Every snag looming in the mist could have been a crouching animal. Once as I straightened up with a handful of sticks I nearly cried out, certain I had seen a bear. I bit my lip, realizing it was only a stump, but my heart took a long while in settling down.

The rain came on before I had started the fire, at first only a thickening of the mist and then a drizzle, as if the clouds we had been breathing all day had suddenly congealed. Jesse and I sat on his rough bench under the awning while rain pattered down, both of us chilled to the bone. He stared out at the circle of blackened stones. "I sure was looking forward to that fire," he muttered.

"We'll have us a fire," I told him.

"How? In the rain?"

"Let me think here a minute." We had brought no paper along except for the map and Jesse's novel and my notebook, and we would shiver all night before sacrificing any of them. Wondering what else we could use for tinder, I remembered a trick my father had taught me. "You ever see any grapevines around here?"

Jesse shut his eyes, thinking, then pointed along the ride. "I believe there's a tangle just off the path to the spring."

"Go see if you can find them, and strip off a wad of the loose bark, and zip it in your driest pocket and bring it back here."

He trudged away through the fine rain and the blue of his jacket soon disappeared among the dark pillars of the trees. Under the makeshift awning I took out my knife and began whittling a stick, letting the curls of wood fall into our frying pan. By the time Jesse returned with a double handful of grapevine bark, I had filled the pan with shavings. I took the stringy bark and rubbed it back and forth between my palms to shred it, and then I added the bark to my pile of shavings.

"Now I need you to hold my jacket over me while I lay the fire," I told him, slipping my arms from the sleeves.

"Use mine," he offered.

"I've been wet before."

I handed him the jacket. Bending over to protect the pan full of tinder from the rain, I stepped out beyond the edge of the awning to kneel over the fire pit. Jesse followed and leaned above me, spreading the jacket like a single flimsy wing to shelter me. I laid the shredded bark in the cinders left by other campers and covered it with the shavings and tilted over them a pyramid of twigs and sticks and cut branches as long and thick as my forearm. Then I drew the match case from my shirt pocket, unscrewed the lid, pulled out a wooden match, struck it along the sandpapery side of the case, and held the flame cupped in my hand. Before I could reach the tinder, the match guttered out, and so did a second one and a third.

"This isn't going to work," Jesse predicted.

"Don't give up yet," I answered, striking a fourth match.

A gust of wind blew out this one, and the next. Rain rattled the jacket over my head and mist blew around me.

"We'll get by," Jesse said.

"We'll get by better with a fire."

I struck another match, encircled it with my palm, reached through a gap in the pyramid of glistening wood and pressed the flame into the nest of bark and shavings. The flame wavered, licking up into the cone of twigs, but would spread no farther without more air. I tilted my face and bent down until my cheek nearly grazed the blackened stones and blew gently. A few twigs caught, but they glowed only so long as I kept puffing at them. When I stopped for a breath the flame sank down.

"We need something to fan it with," I said.

"All right," Jesse answered, "but as soon as I move the rain's going to put it out."

"Just be quick. I'll keep it covered."

I stooped over the faltering fire with my eyes closed against the smoke. Steam hissed from the wet wood and rain drummed on my back. After a few moments of rummaging about under the awning, Jesse returned and nudged me aside. I backed out of the smoke and squinted up to see him waving at the fire with his thick novel encased in a plastic bag. Flames quickly ran up the twigs and wound among the sticks. I laid on a few more branches from our pile.

"Don't smother it," he said.

I started to ask him whose fire he thought this was, anyway, but I held back, remembering that we were on his ground, following his trail, and that I had accepted him as the leader on this journey. He'd earned the right, as a veteran in these mountains and as a boy grown up into his man's body.

I stepped back under the awning. "Let me know when you want me to fan for a while."

By the time he offered me a turn the flames were leaping and there was no need for any more fanning. Shivering, we pulled on dry clothes and sat again on the bench with shoulders touching and stared at the flames until our shivers died down. Smoke mixed with steam and rain to cloud the air. The last remnants of light drained from the sky. Soon there was nothing to see but the fire seething and sparks flying up.

"You hungry yet?" Jesse asked.

"I could eat anything that won't eat me," I answered.

He cooked, I fed the fire. We ate slowly, talking of the day, and then I washed up. Rain dripped from the edges of our lean-to, but the heat from the fire enfolded us against the evening chill. I took out the notebook and wrote my own version of the day in a crooked scrawl. Jesse pulled back his lank hair and bound it in place with an elastic band stretched across his forehead. He propped a small flashlight over his right ear and tucked the butt of it up under the elastic band, then switched on the light and tilted it down so that it shone on the pages of his book.

"You look like a miner," I said.

When he glanced at me, the flashlight dazzled my eyes. "What's that?"

"Never mind. I'm just talking."

"You never run short of words," he observed with a smile, then returned to his reading.

No, I never run short of words, but finding the right ones and yoking them together into sentences that ring true and laying out sentences page after page into a necessary order is always a struggle. To say the simplest thing may baffle me. No piling on of words can ever fully tell how much I love my son, my daughter, my wife, how much I honor my students, how much I exult in this world we briefly share.

"Good fire we built," Jesse said after a while. He switched off the flashlight, pulled it from his headband, and sat staring into the flames. "Even the rain won't put it out."

"Not unless it rains a lot harder," I said.

The two of us watched embers fade and glow as the wind breathed on them. The smell of wet ashes mixed with the smell of burning sap. Rain rattled on the stretched skin of my poncho overhead and hissed as it struck the coals. The sound set me humming.

"You like these mountains?" Jesse asked.

"I do."

"I don't know why, but the mountains make me believe we can change." His dark eyes mirrored the fire. "Maybe not everybody. But at least enough people to start us in a new direction."

"Keep on believing that," I told him, "and you're halfway there."

The fire kept stilling our tongues. Flames whipped from the tops of burning sticks like orange flags. Sparks rose into the dark and dwindled to the size of stars and winked out, and new sparks followed. An old patched-together prayer rose in me:

> My God, my God, my holy one, my love,
> May I be open and balanced and peaceful.

I breathed in with the first line, breathed out with the second, and that breathing seemed to me the whole of the story we the living have to tell.

TED KOOSER

Treehouse

Because my son would soon graduate from college and move many miles away, I'd gotten very busy with my hands. The orderly world of our lives together was spinning out of control, and I spent nearly all of my free time compulsively fixing, straightening, sorting and resorting things.

My first wife and I were divorced when Jeff was two, and he'd grown up with her in Iowa, visiting me in the summers and on holidays. Then he came to Nebraska to finish college, and he'd been living with my wife and me for the past three years. It had been the best time of our lives, having him near.

During that time, he had set about to make the farm his own. He had fixed up a little apartment in one of our outbuildings, and had even put an old washtub on the rafters so that he could drain a little water into a makeshift sink. He spent most of his time down there in his fancy corncrib, his music thudding against the walls, his computer humming.

He organized the innards of the garage and workshop in the barn in his own fashion, putting the tools where he could find them, nailing up makeshift shelves here and there, sorting the cans of nails by size. Soon he knew where everything was and I knew where nothing was, but I didn't resent it. These years were my opportunity to be a full-time father, and I enjoyed the disruption.

Now, in my anguish about his going away, I was beginning to make things worse for both of us by starting to disassemble his order to re-impose my own. I could have waited until he was gone, but I was beside myself. I began to straighten the corners he'd found for himself.

On one chilly Saturday while he was in Iowa to visit his girlfriend, I started the day by standing in the shelter of the barn door sizing up his old treehouse. I wanted to tear it down in the worst way. He and a friend had built it one summer—a crazy, catty-wampus collection of old boards, window screens, and plywood slung between a clump 167 of three old ash trees. The summer they'd built it they'd slept out there for weeks. It was their place on our place, and it had become for me a central symbol of Jeff's place in my life, and of all the happiness we'd shared. Now I wanted to tear it to splinters. I wanted to pull it apart and throw the nails in every direction. I wanted to burn it alive where it sat in the trees.

But first I diverted my energy to a big pile of used bricks that the former owner of our farm had left behind. It was a job that I had asked Jeff to do several times and that he had started and left unfinished. Now I was going to do it myself. The treehouse watched over my shoulder.

Spring had come to our country place, and the wild plum bushes were in flower. If you stood close enough to take in their perfume, you could hear the bees at work. I worked like a bee at a flower, fierce with concentration. I neatly stacked the good bricks and then loaded up my old pickup with the broken ones and threw them one by one—threw them hard—into a washed-out place on our grassland to the west. That took all morning, a few hours of the time before the day upon which my son would be leaving us for good.

The treehouse was still there when I drove back down the drive. It floated above the property, gray as a storm cloud, radiating sentiment. I walked over and stood in its shadow.

The boys had done a good job of building it, fitting the scrap boards together, nailing on roofing material to keep it dry, but it was not so well-built that one crazed father with a crowbar couldn't tear it all down in a weekend, leaving no trace.

A breeze had come up during the morning and the trees tugged at the boards, making the joints cry out. Stealthily, I climbed the steps that had been nailed onto one of the supporting trees, and peered inside. The space was empty except for a few cow bones in one corner that the boys had found and put there years before. I crawled inside and lay down on the floor, looking up at the roof. This was the way in which the two boys had seen the world, I thought. They had lain here and looked up as the nights darkened and the coyotes barked and the oppressive adults slept in their bed in the house. This was how it had felt to be Jeff, once, long ago, when he was a boy. I closed my eyes and listened to the creaking boards and the breezes whistling softly in the branches. I felt the treehouse move just slightly as the wind pushed the trees one way and then another. Tears came to my eyes.

Today, the treehouse still floats in the arms of its trees. Some of the roof has pulled open, and rain will eventually rot out the floor. The steps going up the trunk are loose, and I have to warn visiting children to be careful climbing up. I hear them up there talking softly about the mysterious cow bones, wondering who left them.

CODA

LORRAINE ANDERSON

Watermarks and Bloodlines

Oh never fear death for me for I have looked at the
earth and loved it. I have been part of earth's beauty
in moments beyond the edge of living.
PEGGY POND CHURCH, "I Have Looked at the Earth"

My father's topo map of Sequoia and General Grant National Parks is
tawny with age, its crease lines tattered with folding and unfolding.
The blue lines denoting the rivers—the South Fork Kings River, Roaring River, Bubbs Creek—remind me of the thick blue veins that used
to stand out on the backs of his weathered hands when grasping the
cork handle of a fishing pole, reeling in the line after a bite. Those blue-
veined hands offered sturdy support when his wife and four kids—two
sons, two daughters—followed him in jumping some brook across a
Sierra trail.

My family spent its vacations the first nine summers of my life, the
better part of the fifties, camping in Cedar Grove, now a portion of
Kings Canyon National Park immediately north of Sequoia. I remember the scent of incense cedar in the sunshine, clear blue skies above
towering trees, the roaring of rivers, thunderstorms that turned the
campground roads into streams, my father returning at dusk with dinner in his wicker fishing creel. These memories go deep in the blood.

A few weeks before my father died, as we were sitting at the table after he had struggled to eat three or four bites of the dinner my mother
had prepared, he described a moment fifty years earlier in Kings
Canyon that had come back to him so clearly he could smell and feel it.
"I still remember that morning," he said softly, half to himself. A youth
of twenty-four, he had gotten up at five and set out across Zumwalt
Meadows to fish the Kings River. Something about the dawn light or
the moist chill of the air or the pine and cedar resin on the breeze had
so pierced him to the heart that the mark had become indelible.

My father never made much of himself in conventional terms. He
was not good military material, though he joined the Navy in 1940. 173

He learned Morse code and was stationed as a telegraph operator at Eureka on the coast of northern California. Sunday, December 7, 1941, was a fine day, and he had the radio watch that morning. As he told it in a brief reminiscence he typed up in 1986, "The communications room was in the back of the administration building, facing the ocean. About 9:00 I climbed through the ground floor window and took a stroll along the beach." There he was, gazing lazily out at the Pacific instead of being at his post as the Japanese bombed Pearl Harbor. With radio traffic coming in fast and heavy, he was able to climb back in the office window all but unnoticed by the communications officer.

One time I asked my father what his favorite sound was. "The Kings River at full spring flood," he replied without hesitation. Though he had other enthusiasms—raising chickens, horse racing, a fascination with flying that sprang from his teenage adulation of Charles Lindbergh, stamp and coin collecting, his pint-sized dog Poppi—none of them went as deep as his love of the waters of the Range of Light. This was his genius.

My father did blue-collar work most of his life, except for a brief stint as an insurance agent, an occupation for which he was entirely unsuited. At midlife, in the early sixties, he yielded to the lure of those Sierra waters and moved our family from the Bay Area to the north shore of Lake Tahoe. He was following his bliss before Joseph Campbell began urging burned-out American strivers to do so. Though he had to work as a janitor in a casino and drive a school bus to make ends meet, he had left behind the daily grind of commuting by freeway to a job at a South San Francisco industrial plant, something he'd done for nearly two decades. On his rare days off, we all hiked in the woods.

Recently, a friend of mine has been grieving that her father, a doctor, never shared moments in nature with her. I have other friends whose successful fathers—airline pilot, lawyer, businessman—never took them camping or hiking. I was surprised the first time I realized that not everyone grew up in such an easy relationship with wild nature as I did. Wasn't time spent in nature the foundation of every family's life? No. How sad. How ominous.

Whatever his failings were, my father did this thing right: He loved a place on Earth passionately, and he shared that love with his children. That's the legacy that matters most to me, and I think he understood this. He left my mother and each of his children a handwritten note with his will. To me he wrote: "My heart sings with joy for the outdoors: the woods, the meadows, the mountains, trails, trees, scents, birds, flowers, and fresh clean air. All these we have shared. How wonderful."

When my father received the diagnosis of cancer of the esophagus, it was Thanksgiving. My brothers and I and our assorted partners and children were visiting him and my mother at their house outside Carson City, Nevada, where they had moved from Tahoe after retirement. We sat down to talk about what he was going to do, and he declared that if he could only go live in the woods, he would outlive all the doctors. I said, "Then you must do that. You must." He didn't.

Instead he underwent chemotherapy and did small woodworking projects in the garage between mealtimes that became a battle between his mind and his body as he struggled to get food down past the tumor. Always lean, he quickly became emaciated. Casting about for some way to motivate him to live, I proposed a Father's Day get-together in Kings Canyon. This was February. He sent me a Valentine's card, an uncharacteristic gesture, in which he wrote: "Last night lying in bed I was planning on where to fish the Kings River in June." He died on the last day of April.

Many times during those last months, he admitted to me, he thought about walking out the door and heading west, through the sagebrush and up the steep eastern flank of the Sierra and into the sky. "Just take me up on the mountain and leave me in a snowbank," he said on Easter weekend when I was visiting. "Row me out in Lake Tahoe and push me overboard," he pleaded as his dying stretched out grimly before him.

"I love water," he mused as he sat down with me at the lunch table with a small bottle of mineral water in his hand that Easter weekend. "I mean water running in rivers, in the mountains. Think of me when you sit beside a mountain stream." When I drove up from the Sacramento Valley three weeks later to spend his final days with him, the first thing he asked me from his bed was, "How was the American River running along Highway 50?" The winter of 1992–93 had been a wet one after a six-year drought, and at the end of April the river was running high.

Once, as my brother and I pulled him up into a sitting position so he could take a drink, I was startled by the clear, deep blue of his eyes, like Lake Tahoe on a cold, still winter afternoon. In his last days as he lay uncomfortably in bed, shifting restlessly, I wanted more than anything else for those eyes to be able to see the springtime green that was coming over the vast land outside the house. The sun was thawing the frozen earth and the mountains were melting into music, as John Muir had put it.

My father died of dehydration. When he became unable to swallow liquid anymore, his earlobes shriveled like dried apricots and his body started its final shutting down. I was alone with him when he stopped breathing. The spirit that had been marked so indelibly by water in the mountains was suddenly gone. But outside, the immense green flank of the Sierra ran with a million rivulets as the eternal wheel of the seasons turned once more.

Lorraine Anderson is a freelance writer and editor with a special interest in nature and women's experience. Her essay "Watermarks and Bloodlines" was previously published in *Terra Nova* (MIT Press, 1998, copyright © by Lorraine Anderson, reprinted by permission of Lorraine Anderson). She has edited *Sisters of the Earth*, *Literature and the Environment* (with Scott Slovic and John P. O'Grady), and *At Home on This Earth: Two Centuries of U.S. Women's Nature Writing* (with Thomas S. Edwards). She has a master's degree in creation spirituality from Naropa University.

John Bower studies evolutionary questions in animal communication—an interest that combines his love of music (urban roots in Rochester, New York) with his love of nature (summers spent on his grandparents' dairy farm in rural upstate New York). He teaches courses in evolution, field ecology, natural history, ornithology, field audio recording, digital audio mixing, and folk music performance at Fairhaven College, a small interdisciplinary student-centered college within Western Washington University. He lives partway up the westward slope of a hill in Bellingham, Washington, where he delights in the Pacific Northwest birds, weather, and light with his partner, two young children, and his dog.

Brian Doyle is the editor of *Portland Magazine* at the University of Portland in Oregon. He is the author of *77 Saints*, a collection of "brief excitable headlong essays" about Catholic saints; *Credo*; and with his father, Jim Doyle, *Two Voices*, a collection of their essays. *Two Voices* won a Christopher Award and a Catholic Press Association Book Award. Doyle's essay "Eating Dirt" appeared in *Orion* in 1998. He has also published essays in *American Scholar*, *Atlantic Monthly*, *Commonweal*, and *Harper's*. His essays have been reprinted in the *Best American Essays* anthologies of 1998 and 1999, in *Best Spiritual Writing* 1999, 2001, and 2002, and in the anthologies *Thoughts of Home*, *Family*, *In Brief*, and *Resurrecting Grace*. Doyle reviews books for the *San Francisco Chronicle*, the *Oregonian*, and *Preservation* magazine; is an essayist for the *Age* newspaper in Melbourne, Australia; and is recipient of the *American Scholar's* Best Essay Award in 2000, for an essay on Plutarch.

John Elder has taught at Middlebury College since 1973. During that time, his wife, Rita, and he have raised their three children in the mountain village of Bristol, Vermont. His essay "Pillow and Cradle" is an excerpt from *Reading the Mountains of Home* (Harvard University Press, copyright © 1998 by the President and Fellows of Harvard College, reprinted by permission of the publisher), in which Elder explores the character of his family's home landscape through the lens of Robert Frost's poem "Directive." The essays in his most recent book, *The Frog Run*, connect the wholeness of nature and culture in Vermont with three other topics: proposals to expand the acreage preserved as wilderness; a continuous literary lineage grounded in the Psalms; and the living rural tradition associated with making maple syrup.

Mark Harfenist grew up in the suburbs of New York, where he was, all else aside, a delinquent, a runaway, a dropout, and a dedicated, all-purpose Angry Young Man. He lived in a variety of places under an assortment of circumstances prior to settling six years ago in Bellingham, Washington, at the foot of the Cascade Mountains. Indoor spaces have always made him chafe and squirm. Harfenist has spent much of his life living, working, and playing in the out-of-doors, and much of that time in the mountains on a number of continents. During most of his adult life he has done one sort of physical labor or another, so it is with a sense of wonder (sometimes leavened with fret and worry) that he now finds himself about to graduate from college at the age of forty-six. He has never been skilled at following the usual rules or at conforming to the desires and expectations of others, although he has made great strides in this realm in recent years. Harfenist continues to hope that, all evidence to the contrary, he will someday learn moderation in the use of that noblest of punctuation marks, the semicolon.

Bernd Heinrich grew up in a forest in northern Germany and on farms in western Maine. He received his BA and MS from the University of Maine in Orono, and a PhD from UCLA, all in zoology. Since early childhood, Heinrich has had close contact with insects and birds—collecting, caring for as pets, watching and researching, photographing, and sketching and writing about them. He was a professor of entomology at the University of California, Berkeley, before returning home to the East to be professor of biology at the University of Vermont in 1980.

Ted Kooser's most recent collection of poems is *Winter Morning Walks: 100 Postcards to Jim Harrison*. "Treehouse" appears in his book of personal essays *Local Wonders: Seasons in the Bohemian Alps* (University of Nebraska, copyright © 2002 by the University of Nebraska Press, reprinted by permission of the publisher).

Gretchen Legler is an associate professor of creative writing in the Humanities Department at the University of Maine at Farmington, specializing in non-fiction writing. She has also taught nonfiction writing in the MFA program at the University of Alaska, Anchorage, and in many community venues. Prior to her life in academia, Legler spent time working as a forest ranger with the U.S. Forest Service in Utah and Wyoming, and as an agricultural journalist in North Dakota. Her essay "Fishergirl" was previously published in her first book, *All the Powerful Invisible Things: A Sportswoman's Notebook* (Seal Press, copyright © 1995 by Gretchen Legler, reprinted by permission of the publisher). Essays from that collection have won two Pushcart Prizes, and have been widely excerpted and anthologized in venues including *Orion, Uncommon Waters, Another Wilderness, Gifts of the Wild, Minnesota Seasons*, and *A Different Angle*. Legler's scholarly work on American women nature writers and eco-criticism has appeared in journals and anthologies including *Studies in the Humanities* and *Interdisciplinary Studies in Literature and the Environment*. She is currently at work on a book of essays about Antarctica, where she spent six months in 1997 as a fellow with the National Science Foundation's Artists and Writers Program. Her creative nonfiction about Antarctica has most recently appeared in *Orion* and in the *Women's Review of Books*.

Charles W. Luckmann lives with his family (Susan, Arielle, and Noah) in Bellingham, Washington. He is the department chair of Languages and Literature at Skagit Valley College.

Stephen J. Lyons is the author of *Landscape of the Heart*, a single father's memoir, which included his essay "The Eagles of Beauty Bay" (Washington State University Press, 1996, reprinted by permission of the publisher). His prose and poetry has appeared in many anthologies, including *Passionate Hearts, Split Verse, Bless the Day, Living in the Runaway West*, and *In Black and White: Idaho Photography and Writing*. He writes full-time from his home in the rural Midwest.

Jessica Maxwell's essay "Her Father's Daughter" was published previously in *Audubon* in 1993. An NEA Creative Writing Fellow and former *Esquire* travel writer, Maxwell created and wrote *Audubon* magazine's "True Nature" conservation column until she was offered a book deal she couldn't refuse—to write about her love of rivers and wild fish. *I Don't Know Why I Swallowed the Fly* was published in 1997; the same year saw the publication of a collection of her magazine travel stories, *Femme d'Adventure*; then the year 2000 brought about the publication of her reluctant tale of learning to play golf, *Driving Myself Crazy*. Her work has been included in numerous anthologies, including Bill Bryson's *Best American Travel Writing of 2000*. She lives in Eugene, Oregon—with her husband and part-bobcat kitty—where she is at work on a spiritual adventure book that includes an expanded version of "Her Father's Daughter."

James McKean teaches English and creative writing at Mount Mercy College in Cedar Rapids, Iowa. He has published two books of poems, *Headlong* and *Tree of Heaven*. *Headlong* won a Great Lakes Colleges Association's New Writer Award for Poetry, and *Tree of Heaven* won a 1994 Iowa Poetry Prize. "Recoveries" is one of a series of essays McKean is writing about athletics in his family and playing basketball. From 1964 to 1968, he played basketball for Washington State University in Pullman, Washington, in what was then the Pac-8 Conference. He was an All-Coast selection his junior and senior years. McKean earned graduate degrees from the University of Iowa's Writers' Workshop and the English Department.

Mark Menlove now lives at 9,200 feet in Utah's Wasatch Mountains with his wife, Dana, son Asa, and, as often as possible, son Logan. His writing has appeared in several national and regional periodicals and is anthologized in *Living in the Runaway West*—which features the best essays of *High Country News*'s syndicated "Writers on the Range"—and in *Witness*, a collection of Utah writers. "The Sound of Water" is an excerpt from a memoir in progress.

Paul S. Piper is a teaching librarian at Western Washington University as well as a writer. He has published two chapbooks of poetry, and poetry, fiction, and nonfiction in a variety of magazines, journals, and books. His essay "Around the Next Bend" was published previously in *Northern Lights* in 2000. Piper has always had the philosophy of living where he'd vacation, which has taken him to long stints in Montana, Hawaii, and now the Pacific Northwest. Over the years he has been involved in numerous conservation and wilderness efforts.

His involvement as a father dates back to the birth of his son, Jordan, in 1986. He has also been involved with the men's movement in various ways.

John Rember was born in Sun Valley, Idaho, and raised north of there in Sawtooth Valley. He studied at Albertson College of Idaho and Harvard University, and has worked as a ski patrolman, Forest Service wilderness ranger, cement worker, bartender, medical writer, and college professor. Rember is currently an associate professor of English and journalism and the honors director at Albertson College of Idaho. His essay "Traplines" also appears in his newest book, *Memory Tricks* (Pantheon, 2003). Rember is a contributing writer for *Skiing* magazine, and he has published two previous books: *Coyotes in the Mountains* and *Cheerleaders from Gomorrah*.

Scott Russell Sanders was born in Tennessee and grew up in Ohio. He studied at Brown University before going on, as a Marshall Scholar, to complete a PhD in English literature at Cambridge University. In 1971 he joined the faculty of Indiana University, where he is distinguished professor of English and where he directs the Wells Scholars Program. He has published eighteen books, including novels, collections of stories and essays, and personal narratives, as well as seven storybooks for children. His essay "Mountain Music IV" was previously published in *Hunting for Hope: A Father's Journeys* (Beacon Press, 1998, copyright © 1998 by Scott Russell Sanders, reprinted by permission of Beacon Press, Boston), a book that explores the sources for healing and renewal. His most recent books are *The Country of Language*, a brief memoir of experiences that have shaped his life as a writer, and *The Force of Spirit*, meditations on the sacred in everyday life. For his collected work in nonfiction, Sanders was honored in 1995 with a Lannan Literary Award. He and his wife, Ruth, a biochemist, have reared two children in their home town of Bloomington, Indiana.

David Sobel, MEd, is the director of Teacher Certification Programs in the Education Department and co-director of the Center for Environmental Education at Antioch New England Graduate School. He was one of the founders of the Harrisville Children's Center and has served on the board of public and private schools. Sobel is a member of the editorial board of the journal *Encounter: Education for Meaning and Social Justice* and is a field correspondent for *Orion Afield*. His published books include *Children's Special Places*, *Beyond Ecophobia: Reclaiming the Heart in Nature Education*, and *Mapmaking with Children: Sense of Place Education for the Elementary Years*. In 1991, he won an Education Press Award. Sobel is currently co-director of Project CO-SEED (Community-based School Environmental Education). This project creates partnerships between communities, school districts, and environmental organizations. Sobel's exploration and documentation of the natural interests of children are the foundation for much of his work. He has served as a consultant with school districts, environmental organizations, and the National Park Service to assist educators with curriculum development and program planning from a learner-centered perspective. Sobel relishes the opportunity to go on natural world adventures with his own children.

Frank Stewart is the author of four books, including *A Natural History of Nature Writing*, and the editor of eight anthologies concerned with the literature and natural history of Asia and the Pacific. He is also the editor of *Mānoa: A Pacific Journal of International Writing*. He has received the Whiting Writers Award and the Elliot Cades Award for Literature. Stewart lives part-time on the island of Oahu, where he teaches at the University of Hawaii, and part-time on the Hamakua Coast of Hawaii's Big Island. He has two daughters, Chloe and Emma.

Stan Tag lived his earliest years near the confluences of the Blackfoot, the Clark Fork, and the Bitterroot Rivers, in a valley ringed with mountains marked by a succession of ancient lakeshores. He spent his youth living on the urban edges of the fire-charred, mud-sliding, smog-filled, dry and verdant hills northeast of the City of Angels. He studied literature in a well-groomed forest of ponderosa pines and wrote his dissertation on Maine woods narratives while living on the high ground above three different rivers: the Iowa, the Cannon, and the Boise. Tag lives with his family in a hundred-year-old house—built from old-growth Douglas fir and western red cedar—on a settled plateau between two salmon-running creeks, a short walk from Bellingham Bay, and in the shadow and watchful snowy eye of a volcano. At Fairhaven College he teaches courses in American literature and culture, writing, natural history, and walking. He is completing a book on the nineteenth-century history of Katahdin, Maine's highest mountain.

AMERICAN LAND & LIFE SERIES

The People's Forests
By Robert Marshall

Pilots' Directions: The Transcontinental Airway and Its History
Edited by William M. Leary

Places of Quiet Beauty: Parks, Preserves, and Environmentalism
By Rebecca Conard

Reflecting a Prairie Town: A Year in Peterson
Text and photographs by Drake Hokanson

A Rural Carpenter's World:
The Craft in a Nineteenth-Century New York Township
By Wayne Franklin

Salt Lantern: Traces of an American Family
By William Towner Morgan

Thoreau's Sense of Place: Essays in American Environmental Writing
Edited by Richard J. Schneider